Sid's Way

The Life and Death of Sid Vicious

Keith Bateson and Alan Parker

Acknowledgements

The authors are grateful to the following for their help in the production of this book: Glen Matlock, John 'Boogie' Tiberi, Dave Goodman & Bob Gruen (for help and insight; Edward Christie & Sandra Wake (for their help over the years); Colin & Michelle Kennaugh (without whom...); George Gelleburn & Dave Henderson (Two Primates Talking); Paul Burgess (a fellow traveller); Jon Salisbury, Darren Lee & Julian Weyer Brown; Jon McCaughey (Bridge Street Mafia); Paul Erswell, Dani Gilmore, Ian Tipping & Steve Clark (Boredom); Steve Burch at King George's Hall; Tracie Hamilton at Admiral Print; Goz at Eagles Wings; Paul Truelove at Gecko; Martin Roach at IMP; Bob Ramsey; Andy Huntley at Ver Jam; Wayne Connolly (Happy Days); Chris & Andrew at Omnibus Press; Ian Duckworth; Sue Madigan; Seamus Hefferman at Shamrock; Louise Fowler (Understand Me); Rich Meehan at MTV; Anne Marie Tomlinson (4 Real); finally, mum, dad and David for putting up with it.

Further information on Sid and The Sex Pistols can be obtained from Scott Murphy at The Filth And The Fury, 24 Muirside Street, Ballieston, Glasgow, G69 7EL.

First published ©1991 Omnibus Press
This edition copyright © 1998 Omnibus Press
(A Division of Book Sales Limited)

ISBN: 0.7119-2483-X
Order No: OP

Exclusive Distributors
Book Sales Limited,
8/9 Frith Street,
London W1V 5TZ, UK.

Music Sales Corporation,
257 Park Avenue South,
New York, NY 10010, USA.

The Five Mile Press,
22 Summit Road,
Noble Park,
Victoria 3174, Australia.

To the Music Trade only:
Music Sales Limited,
8/9 Frith Street,
London W1V 5TZ, UK.

Cover designed by Pearce Marchbank

Printed in Great Britain by
Printwise (Haverhill) Limited, Suffolk

Contents

Photo Credits:
Anne Beverley Collection: 4/5, 6/7, 8/9, 10/11, 12/13, 14/15, 16/17, 18/19, 20/21, 22/23, 24/25, 26/27, 80/81; Adrian Boot: 37, 41, 92; EMI Records: 28/29; Bob Gruen: 2, 48 (b), 49 (t), 50, 51 (b), 52 (t&b), 53 (t), 56 (t & b), 59 (b), 92 (b); LFI: 63 (tr), 65, 66 (b), 67 (t), 68 (l), 68/69, 69 (t), 70, 72/73, 73 (tl, tr & bl), 74, 76, 77; Glen Matlock Collection: 33 (tr & bl); Denis O'Regan: 75 (t&b); Palace Pictures: 85, 86/87, 88/89, 90/91; Pictorial Press: 34, 36, 44/45, 59 (t), 63 (b), 64, 66 (t), 67 (b), 68 (t), 69 (b), 71 (t), 78/79, 93, 96; Barry Plummer: 32 (t), 35; Retna: 42/43, 48 (t), 55 (t&b), 85, 62 (b); Rex Features: 30 (bottom), 32 (bottom), 40, 51, 53 (bottom), 54, 60/61, 62 (top); Joe Stevens: 57 (t), John Tiberi: 33 (br), 63 (tl), 82, 84; Virgin Records: 39; Warner Brothers Records: 30, 31 (t&b), 46/47.

Every effort has been made to trace the copyright holders of the photographs in this book but one or two were unreachable. We would be grateful if the photographers concerned would contact us.

A catalogue record for this book is available from the British Library.
Visit Omnibus Press on the web at www.omnibuspress.com

Introduction

Sid's Way was first published by Omnibus Press in 1991 and this new edition has been produced to mark the 20th Anniversary of Sid's death which will occur in 1999. It's impossible to imagine what Sid might have felt about The Sex Pistols today. They are, of course, a flourishing concern; not quite as flourishing as Pink Floyd or The Rolling Stones - to name two groups that the Pistols set out to destroy - but flourishing nevertheless in the same way that rock legends of every era nowadays prosper by drinking from the cup of nostalgia.

It was all very different when Sid, the Pistols' second bass player, was in the band. Their whole philosophy seemed to have been based on the concept of an instant group that would explode when it became successful, and that when that stage had been reached there was no point continuing. The group's brief career was an artistic statement in itself, and what was left behind - the records, film clips, pictures - merely by-products.

At least that's how Sid probably viewed it. No-one can be sure of course, just as no-one knows exactly what happened in the Chelsea Hotel in October of 1978, but the facts are here, along with our thoughts on how Simon Beverley became Sid Vicious and ended up dead at the age of 21.

The original idea behind this book was born in the summer of 1989, when Anne Beverley and I decided that the time was ripe for a book about her son, and it was always our intention to include less of the Sid the fans read about and more of the Simon they didn't. The first draft of the original manuscript didn't please everyone; Anne thought it too revealing, the publishers thought it was bland. The final manuscript was eventually translated into Japanese which pleased everyone involved.

Over the next few years Anne Beverley and I worked together on a number of radio and CD projects relating to Sid. Although I've worked on many Sex Pistols projects since this book, it's this book that means the most because this is right where we started. If I hadn't been busy in 1990, I doubt I'd be run off my feet in 1998. I have added nothing to it and by the same token taken nothing away. This is just as it was, Sid's Way...

Anne Beverley took her own life on September 6, 1996, and this book is dedicated to her and Deborah Spungen.

Alan Parker, June 1998.

1

Sun, sea and childhood: Ibiza and the early years

Ibiza is the southernmost of three sunkissed holiday islands, Mallorca, Menorca and Ibiza, which lie off the east coast of Spain, and its climate is ideally suited to the needs of British sunseekers getting away from the trials, tribulations and stresses of modern living. For Anne Beverley and her three-year-old son Simon, a trip to Ibiza in 1960 was planned as the holiday of a lifetime but in actuality it turned out to be a nightmare of debt, creditors and the break-up of her relationship with Simon's father, John Ritchie.

John and Anne lived together on the ground floor of a house in Lee Green, near Lewisham in south east London, and, on May 10, 1957, Anne gave birth to John's son. He was christened John Simon Ritchie.

John Ritchie and Anne Beverley parted shortly after Simon was born and as a result Anne was left to bring up her son largely on her own. While Anne Beverley, to this day, refers to her son as Si or Sime, from the time he enters Hackney College of Further Education he will be referred to as Sid.

In his early years Simon was the image of his father but as far as his musical ability was concerned, he owed it all to his mother. Their semi-basement flat in Lee Green had

Anne Beverley with her son, Simon, and Simon's father John Ritchie.

French windows at the back which opened on to a vast jungle of a garden and a small paved patio which served as Simon's play area from the age of 10 months. There was nothing he liked better than to create an unholy racket by playing drums with the two wooden spoons and pans that his mother had given him.

Anne has always been keen on jazz and a fan of Ella Fitzgerald in particular, and her renditions of various Ella classics, especially 'That Old Black Magic', echoed around the small flat and into Simon's consciousness. Anne can remember how their next door neighbour, an Italian lady, rushed in one day completely dumbfounded at the sight and sound of two-year-old Simon toddling around the patio singing 'That Old Black Magic' complete with Ella Fitzgerald's intonations and phrasing.

Anne had very definite views on the terminology of childhood; she was quite prepared at a very early age to react to children in their own way. If her baby said 'goo-goo', she would say 'goo-goo' back because it encouraged him to make sounds. On the other hand, once her child was old enough to apply reasoning, it was far better to call things by their proper names.

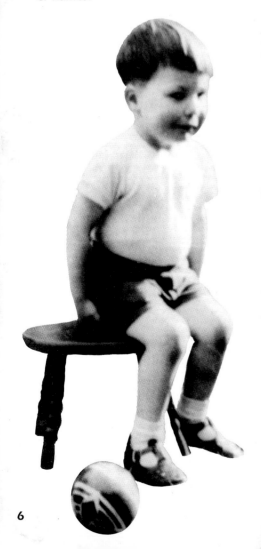

More snapshots from Anne Beverley's family album.

"I remember taking Sime to see his grandparents in Dagenham," says Anne. "That's John's (Ritchie) mum and dad. We went by bus... he'd be about two-years-old. He'd always point to things and say what's that; now I don't believe in baby talk, if you see a cow, don't call it a 'moo-moo', it's a cow; so we were going along and he stood up in his seat and demanded 'What's that?' I said, 'It's a telescopic gasometer,' because that's what it was. So he looked at me and I said it again. He thought about it for a minute and slowly said, 'Oh... tell-iscopic-gas-ommitter!' All the people on the bus looked up. A few months later we went to see his grandparents again and when we passed the same place he piped up, 'Look mum... the telescopic gasometer' for all the world to hear."

Simon was three-years-old when he and Anne went to Ibiza on their eagerly anticipated extended summer holiday. The plan was that John Ritchie would fly out to join them eventually and in the meantime periodically send chunks of money to fund their stay. This part of the arrangement failed to materialise. "I should have been suspicious at the time, one way tickets only," says Anne in somewhat rueful hindsight.

They stayed in Ibiza town itself and both of them, at first anyway, enjoyed the sun, sea and sand of what was then a relatively unspoilt Mediterranean island. One of Simon's earliest social experiences was discovering the abrasive characteristics of Ibizan children; all flying hands, flailing fists and Catalan invective. The belligerence of the children on the island forced Simon into a close attachment with his mother.

"He'd never leave my side," she recalls. "If I went to the loo he'd have to come in with me otherwise he'd bang on the door and cry. People we knew quite well would offer to look after him, you know, just down the road, still in sight, but no way. Having said that, he'd strike up conversations with any adult."

Anne can also recall an evening dinner party that took place in the countryside round Ibiza. While the hostess was in the kitchen, Anne, a friend and the host were in the lounge listening to modern jazz on the record player. Simon, meanwhile, was making himself at home in the kitchen with the hostess. "The girl popped in from the kitchen to enquire as to whether we wanted more drinks and I decided to check on Si to see if he was bothering the hostess. Seems he'd developed a liking for orange curaçao, and had drank two or three glasses of the stuff. Apart from being one over the eight, he was as good as gold... so much so that he went into one of his extemporisation routines to the jazz records that the grown-ups were listening to."

This wasn't the only occasion during the holiday that Simon showed an early interest in alcohol which caused much embarrassment and mirth.

"We were wandering round by the harbour and Si wanted a drink, so I sent him along to Pepe's bar. He was one of our friends and I knew he'd come to no harm. He ran off, turning and waving every few yards or so, because that's what he was like. About 10 minutes later he returned in tears. My immediate reaction was, who's hit you or whatever. Si told me that Pepe wouldn't give him a drink. Well, you know what I'm like; wouldn't give you a drink, wouldn't he? We'll soon see about that."

When Anne Beverley tackled the bar owner Pepe about it, it seems that Simon had marched into the bar and said "Ola Pepe, tiene-usted un cerveza, por favor?" and Pepe had replied "Naranjada, no cerveza por los Chicos!" That had been the problem. Simon had asked for a beer and Pepe had said no, orange for little boys. It seems that even the flexible Spanish licensing laws draw the line at serving beer to three-year-olds.

On another occasion Anne, a friend and Simon had dined out in an expensive restaurant, a celebratory meal throughout which Simon had been as good as gold. Brandy and liqueurs were ordered by the grown up members of the party but young Simon Ritchie demanded brandy also. Anne, in turn described it as alcoholic, nasty, not for little boys, and definitely not allowed. Children's logic prevailed: "If it's nasty why are you drinking it. If you're having it why can't I?"

Anne Beverley remembers: "I said, 'OK Simon if you want a brandy, you shall have one. You're bugging everyone. But if I get you one, you'll damn well drink it.' OK says Si, in other words, the bet's on. This enormous brandy arrived, not like an English one, you know, damn great tumbler loaded with ice; Si put it to his lips, took a small sip; you could see that he wanted to pull a face but instead he smiled, said, it's lovely, and managed to drink the lot."

Their means of travel around the island was by bicycle; John Ritchie hadn't been forthcoming with money and, in fact, communication between

Simon on holiday with his mother in Ibiza.

him and Anne was almost non-existent. Simon clung to the back of Anne's friend on the pillion seat of a bicycle, totally drunk, strapped on for additional safety and shouting 'Cannelloni' – which he'd had for dinner – all the way home.

Money was extremely tight throughout their stay on Ibiza and Anne became particularly adept at moving from one set of lodgings to another very quickly. She was also helped by the generosity of the largely American contingent of hip, not hippy, people who had made Ibiza their home. However, the once idyllic existence rapidly became fraught with problems until they didn't know where the next peseta was coming from.

The foreign community living in Ibiza had a tendency to give nicknames to friends and acquaintances, and among them was a 70-year-old man who was always referred to as 'Deaf Henry'. One day Simon was with his mother and a party of friends when Henry walked by. "Look mum... there's Dead Henry," Simon shouted to much general amusement.

"Mark my words, Anne, that child will either be the Prime Minister of England or a total dropout," one of Anne's friends predicted.

Eventually the money and credit dried up completely and Anne decided that there was nothing to be gained by remaining in Ibiza any longer. She has never been a person to outstay her welcome.

One of the problems that mother and son were to encounter on their return to England was the unavailability of accommodation. One of Anne's principal concerns was now the 'colourful' language that Simon had picked up from the various 'colourful' people with whom they had associated in Ibiza.

"We decided to go home to my mum," she says. "The thing with John Ritchie had finished anyway and I'd got Simon, if I needed anything to remind me of him. Quite frankly, he'd let us both down, but that's water under the bridge.

"I was so worried that now we were back in straightsville, the little phrases Simon had picked up would go down like a lead balloon. You know things like, 'So I said to this mother-fucker.' He once said to me, 'What does fuck your apple pie mean, mum.' I told him it was just a phrase some people used and it meant they didn't want any apple pie, thank you. A bit tricky at four-years-old. Anyway, on the boat coming home, I suddenly

Simon with CP, the family pet, and Marty, a friend of the family in Ibiza, in 1961.

thought... that's all I need Simon calling Gran a stupid cunt, I think she'd find it all a bit offensive and wonder just how I'd been bringing Simon up. I had a chat with him and, bless him, he never said a wrong word."

Anne and Simon settled back in England with her mother but soon afterwards found accommodation in Balham. The elderly lady who owned the house where they lived rarely went out, so Anne had a conveniently built-in child minder, which enabled her to work long hours at Ronnie Scott's jazz club in Soho. Whilst it was obvious that Anne had to work to survive, she was unwilling to spend long periods away from her son, but since she worked from six p.m. to two a.m. and took a night bus home she was able to spend most of the daylight hours with Simon. She was lucky enough to find a safe haven for Simon for two hours each weekday afternoon at the Rudolph Stein Nursery School, a private fee-paying establishment. Simon loved the atmosphere at the school.

Anne eventually decided that the daily journey from Balham to Soho was unacceptable so, thanks again to her mother's and sister's good graces, she set up home in Drury Lane in a flat which comprised little more than a couple of rooms off a long corridor. The corridor, windowless and covered only with a canopy, was open to the elements, and the rooms themselves had no sanitation and no hot water, just a cold tap and moveable basin. It was lit by gas and the toilets were housed outside, in the concrete block that held up the corridor.

Anne could now, at last, make proper preparation for Simon's early education. His first school was St. Peter and St. Paul in Soho's Great Windmill Street, a neighbourhood best described as cosmopolitan, but which is probably one of the most corrupt, prostitute-ridden square miles in Britain.

"When he got to St. Peter and Paul's he was going through this fidgeting and twitching stage", says Anne Beverley. "All the time you were talking to him, he'd be at it. I'd ask him what he had for lunch and, on the occasions he actually remembered, he'd give me a long list of what had been served and then proceed to tell me what he hadn't eaten; the potatoes were lumpy so I didn't eat them or on other occasions he just wouldn't remember anything. Mind you, I always cooked him a meal at night; looking back, it's perhaps as well, otherwise he'd have starved to 11 death. He did love my cooking though."

Simon's twitching not only affected his concentration at school but also invited victimisation from other pupils. He often came home from school covered in scratches after a difference of opinion with a boy named Lionel.

Lionel was the school bully and, like many bullies before him, was larger than average and apparently suffering from an excess of Y chromosomes which encourage aggressive behaviour. Anne Beverley, never one to fight shy of confrontation if Simon was involved, tackled the school about it, complaining that her son was being victimised by Lionel the Terrible. The school acknowledged the problem but said that allowances had to be made because the boy had seen countless psychiatrists and had a character disorder.

Anne decided that the simplest thing to do would be to remove Simon from this particular school and find another. Eventually she found Farm Street School, well situated in the area around the United States Embassy in Grosvenor Square, which attracted a 'nicer' type of child. It was partly endowed by the nearby church, which had its fair share of society weddings, and therefore its teaching included the Church of England's ethic of 'family and service'. The pupils all wore the correct school uniform of scarlet caps, blazers, ties and grey shorts.

Academically speaking, Simon was a non-starter. He hated all subjects except art and history. The former was attractive to him because it enabled him to do his own thing. Even at this early age his artistic rather than his academic abilities were coming to the fore. Art and painting, along with music, are probably the most subjective forms of self expression and Simon had always been good at expressing himself.

His fondness for history was probably due to the method of teaching employed by his history master who treated the subject more as a series of exciting stories from the past rather than a chronological list of facts to be remembered parrot fashion.

His school reports from Farm Street School describe Simon as 'bright, witty, intelligent but inconsistent in concentration' but his stay at the school was to be short-lived because it was around this time that Anne moved to Oxford where she met and subsequently married Chris Beverley. They had a whirlwind courtship

Ibiza in 1960.

which began in late 1964 and they were married in February 1965, but before Chris could complete the legal proceedings necessary for adopting Simon he died suddenly in August of the same year.

Once again the fighter and the stoic in Anne Beverley surfaced. Life had already brought too many tragedies to let one more setback toss her on to the scrapheap of oblivion. Little did she know that her life would be visited by tragedy after tragedy, each piled remorselessly on top of the other over the next dozen or so years.

They left Oxford for Tunbridge Wells in Kent where, courtesy of Chris Beverley's family, Simon went to a private school run by an old lady who used to be Chris's nanny. It wasn't long before Simon really set the cat amongst the pigeons at this genteel seat of learning by standing up and declaring that he didn't believe in God. It was not that he was a devious child but he had already developed a liking for shocking people.

Simon became a partial boarder at this school and Ma'mselle, Chris's ex-nanny, would have Simon staying at the school during the week and then take him home at weekends to Wadhurst where Chris's mother lived. This arrangement lasted for most of 1966, when Simon was nine-years-old, and Anne was living and working in Tunbridge Wells. Simon's next school was the nearby St. Peter's, a Church of England Primary.

This period of Simon's life – between the ages of nine and 11 – was fairly uneventful and reasonably settled since much of the to-ing and fro-ing had stopped. Anne was left to mourn the loss of her husband and generally get on with the everyday bringing up of an intelligent child. She recalls: "He was Action Man mad; he'd play for hours, humming to himself. He wasn't tidy in your regimented way but at least he'd bung everything into a big metal chest that Ma'mselle had given him. I don't believe in interrupting a child when he's playing with something and is steeped in it. I'd always say, 'Half an hour, Sime,' not... 'Put that away immediately and get to bed.' I believe in discipline but not bullying. It's a pity that Lionel's mother didn't give her delightful son a kick up the jacksie, then perhaps he wouldn't have turned out the way he did.

"He was fine at St. Peter's and then he went to Sandown Court Secondary Modern which he hated. I waved him off every morning and I'd managed to get him and me pedal 13 bikes on HP, so he used his for school and at weekends we used to go riding together."

When Simon reached the age of 12 his mother noticed that he was starting to avoid physical contact with her. Anne assumed that he was reaching puberty and developing his sexuality but that verbally he was still the same loving Simon. She also became aware that the school and teachers seemed very curious as to what Simon's mother was like; evidently Simon's charisma had created this interest.

By 1969 Simon had been at Sandown Court for over a year. It was the year of the moon landing, the end of the sixties was approaching and a new era was about to start. The seventies was to be the last decade that Simon Beverley would know.

The moon flight seems to have been one of the few things to cause dissension during this spell. The school had sent out letters to parents stating that on no account were pupils to stay up to watch the moon landing and, as a result, miss the following day's school.

Anne Beverley: 'I couldn't believe it, one of the most momentous things to happen, ever, and the school was saying they couldn't watch it. Man's first steps on the moon, you mustn't stay up, bollocks! Si said he wanted to watch and I said he could, but it was very late so I sent him to bed at the normal time and got him up to watch it; it was about three o'clock in the morning, I think. Anyway it didn't finish 'till about five o'clock so he was in no fit state to go to school the following day. He'd been a bit worried about what was going to happen at school so I said, 'Forget it Sime. I'll send them a letter'."

The letter left Sandown Court School under no illusions as to what Anne Beverley thought of the idea of depriving her son of the opportunity of watching the moon landing live.

The next stop on the Beverleys never ending itinerary of addresses in the British Isles was at Clevedon, near Bristol, where Simon attended a local secondary school. It was here that Simon ignored his mother for the first time.

"I'd arranged to meet him after school to get him shoes; there he

Anne Beverley's wedding to Chris Beverley, with Simon – as the 'Latchkey Kid' – in the foreground, February 1965.

was, on his bike with all his mates. I know damn well he saw me. Rode straight past me, little sod, but that's how they get at 13, independent and a bit ashamed of having a mummy."

Once again money, or rather lack of it, made the Beverleys return to London, to Stamford Hill, in north east London, not far from Hackney College of Further Education. Here Simon attended Albion Road Secondary Modern. He once confided to his mother that although they'd lived in so many different places, he thought that he was the least screwed up person he knew.

He'd noticed that other kids at Albion Road would keep him waiting on the doorstep when he called round; he wondered what they were afraid of or what they were trying to hide. Anne had managed to get a television by this time, courtesy of Grandma, but after a few months they sold it because, according to Simon, all the other kids could talk about was 'bloody telly'.

Primary and Secondary education complete, Simon left school and decided to earn his living. His first paid employment was at Daks Trousers in Kingsland Road where he began as a general dogsbody and graduated to become a trainee cutter. It was not destined to last.

"He was shown how to cut out pockets and left to get on with it," says Anne. "Apparently you had to clamp down quite a large pile of specially folded pocket material and with a template cut out the pockets with an industrial cutting machine. Simon hadn't clamped properly and consequently the material slipped. The result was that hundreds of pockets were ruined. Simon fell about laughing when he told me... some of the pockets were so small you couldn't even get a thumb in them. Needless to say, Daks fired him."

Simon had a variety of jobs over the next three or four months but these were just stop gaps until he entered Hackney College of Further Education where he had been accepted for a place on an art course.

It was at the Hackney college that he would meet his saviour, champion and eventual destroyer. His name was John Lydon.

2

A boy called Lydon, college and the two Johns

When Sid started at Hackney College of Further Education, Anne Beverley was yet again facing financial worries. This was to be a recurrent problem for the single parent family throughout Simon Beverley's life, but somehow they managed to make ends meet, with little or no help from Simon's father.

Up until this time any rebellious instincts on Simon's part had been suppressed but this would soon change after he entered Hackney College. He'd been very much a loner until this time, privately considering himself a tad superior to most of his contemporaries. At college he met a long haired, skinny, London Irish boy called John Joseph Lydon who would become his soulmate and partner in crime. It is difficult to state with any certainty who influenced who the most: already Sid had begun to experiment with colouring his hair – in emulation of David Bowie – but Lydon had adopted a certain disaffected style which appealed enormously to Sid. They seemed like a matched pair of misfits.

Both considered education to be largely a waste of time and that image and good times were all that mattered.

John Lydon remembers: "At the time I had filthy long hair and I probably looked like a Metallica roadie."

Left: **Simon Beverley, at Hackney College, 1974**

It was around this time that Simon Beverley adopted the nickname of Sid Vicious. "We'd spend a lot of time just sitting around talking about silly names," says Anne Beverley. "You know, just imagine being called Hortense or Imogen. Or blasted Sidney. What a laugh... and we'd genuinely fall about."

Sid's new friend John Lydon had a pet white rat called Sidney and one day at college Simon let John know, in no uncertain terms, what he thought of the name Sidney. As a result John named Simon, Sid. He added Vicious as a contradictory reference to Simon's peaceful character.

"Sid was the least vicious and least screwed up person that I'd ever met then or have met since," he says. "Hence Vicious."

By now Sid had become thoroughly obsessed with rock superstar David Bowie, the androgynous singer/songwriter from Beckenham whose camp image and blurred sexuality was the most exciting thing to happen in the otherwise fairly sterile UK music scene of the early seventies. To Sid, Bowie was the ultimate role model. Bowie posters were plastered all over his bedroom walls, not so much because Sid identified with Bowie's music, but for the outrageous clothes that Bowie chose to drape across his skinny frame. Fashion became an all-important aspect of Sid's life, and the image he projected became crucially important to his relationship with his peers. Bowie was the king of the visual image; his courtiers and admirers followed his lead slavishly, ultimately becoming little more than cardboard cut-outs of their mentor and often six months behind too. Sid saw his way forward by emulating Bowie.

Bowie was the front runner in the glam-rock movement which swamped the UK rock scene in the early seventies. Glam was the antidote to hippy, a reaction against the serious demeanour – and dull outlook – adopted by progressive rockers who rose from the sixties maelstrom with their long, lank hair, flared loon pants and a musical virtuosity which bordered on the obsessive. The music they played was heard most often at great volume in concert or on albums – rarely on singles – and was considered by its aficianados (and perpetrators) to be culturally superior to that of the glam rockers, and thus a generation gap appeared

Sid used his own photograph to create this image of himself while on his photography course at art school.

18

between the progressive rock fans and the glams, the elder siblings against their kid brothers and sisters.

This was the backbone of the kids' music at this time: Bowie in the vanguard with Marc Bolan's T. Rex, graduates of the sixties, wowing the younger female audiences; Roxy Music, the intellectual side of glam, much fêted by critics and the designer band of the day; Slade, rougher and tougher than Bolan on the live stage but definitely down market; and Gary Glitter and Sweet at the bottom of the heap, well packaged but then and now curious novelty items amid the fashion conscious bands of the day.

Meanwhile back at Hackney College the friendship between Sid and John Lydon was blossoming. For a variety of reasons the pair got on like brothers.

John Lydon's rebellious nature could be traced back to the orthodox Irish Roman Catholicism in his family background. He took delight in kicking over the traces by dropping the odd remark about the non-infallibility of the Pope and the non-existence of God, or promoting the case for contraception.

Between Sid and John there was an element of disdain for 'weekenders', those fellow students who dressed and combed their hair in what might best be described as conventional ways during the week but transformed themselves into leery glam rockers for Saturday night. It was a shared contempt they would carry over as punks: the look had to be worn every day, from morning 'till night... it was not a fancy dress costume to be adopted as required and discarded when inappropriate.

Sid Vicious once told his mother: "I can't understand how a group can dress in punk gear on-stage, pretend to be what they're not and then go home in collars and ties."

Sid was also becoming more aware of his own potential as a womaniser and had already started bringing a number of girls home. "There didn't seem any point in trying to prevent this," says Anne. "It was a natural progression. I'd much rather he brought girls home than sneak around some dark back street."

* * *

As the bond between Sid and John strengthened, in another part of London and unknown to them, two like-minded young school mates, Paul Cook and Steve Jones, had already **19** reached the same decision: that formal education was a waste of time.

Instead of attending school they took to visiting their friend Warwick 'Wally' Nightingale's home in West London where they idled away their days drinking beer, smoking and listening to music. While there was nothing in the charts that particularly inspired any of them, they found an affinity with the music of The Who and The Small Faces. It was the early music of these two groups – both London bands who opened their careers in a flurry of aggression – that inspired Wally to form a group to produce original music, albeit loosely based on the kind of music that The Who and The Small Faces once played.

Drums were to be Paul Cook's bag and with much judicious scrimping and scraping he managed to put together a sort of second-hand hybrid Olympic kit. Steve Jones, the self-styled leader of the pack, opted to become the lead singer, and Wally shouldered an electric guitar. Stephen Hayes, another like-minded friend, became the first of many bass guitarists.

Wally and Steve Jones, bereft of funds, had come to the conclusion that the easiest way of obtaining equipment for the group was simply to steal it. Their most notable heist was to rip off David Bowie's gear following the carrot-topped-one's show at the Hammersmith Odeon. The backstage loading bay was but a few moments' walk away from Riverside Studios which the group would soon colonise as a rehearsal studio and where the cache might be stored with some measure of security.

"I lived near Hammersmith Odeon and knew it like the back of my hand," recalls Jones. "Bowie was doing his Ziggy Stardust thing and was booked for a long run. Anyway, after the first night we knew that all the group's gear would be left on-stage, set up ready for the next performance. We waited until the second or third day and sneaked into the theatre. The security bloke was asleep in the stalls so we just dashed out onto the stage and nicked whatever we could move."

Unfortunately this gear, belonging as it did to the hottest star in the London glam galaxy, was as well known as a stolen Van Gogh might have been to the art market. Consequently their original idea of selling it and buying their own equipment with the proceeds was abandoned. Like its real owner, it was too hot to handle and

Left & below left: **Examples of Sid's art work at 17.**

the only alternative was for the newly formed group to use it for their own rehearsals and, ultimately, performances. It was, after all, very impressive gear for a group of absolute beginners such as Cook, Jones, Wally and the ever-changing squad of bass players who followed the incompetent Stephen Hayes. The next one was Paul Cook's brother-in-law Del Noone.

The next problem the group faced was to find adequately soundproofed space in which to rehearse regularly. After trooping around various rooms and cellars they found an upstairs room at 533 King's Road and settled there to bash away with Steve on guitar and vocals, Wally on guitar, Paul on drums and Del on bass. One day Wally Nightingale actually taped a live session but unfortunately times were tight and the tape was used for a Pretenders' album dub at some later date.

Rehearsals continued though competence was slow in coming.

* * *

Sid, aged 17.

By this time the newly christened Sid and his mate John had both dropped out of college. Sid's education had not been entirely wasted as he had grasped certain basic essentials of art and design, and he could draw with some confidence.

John's 'filthy long hair' had by now been hacked short and dyed green as a foil for Sid's equally eye-catching red streaks. This proved too much for the Lydon family and to preserve his independence John had been obliged to leave home.

There was a glut of untenanted property in London at this time and John and Sid found little difficulty in finding a squat in Camden. "We'd decided to give each other some breathing space," says Anne Beverley. "I had an 11th floor council flat which I loved. It was spacious and light and at last I had my own furniture. Sime was getting to that age when we'd find ourselves snapping at each other for the slightest thing."

Sid was still preoccupied with David Bowie. "He was still well impressed with Bowie," says Lydon. "He was mortally in love with the whole Bowie thing. To get his hair to spike at the front he used to hang upside down in a gas oven for hours. I had to time him. 'Sid, 20 minutes is up... it should be sticking up by now.' 'No, it ain't you liar,' says Sid. He'd got serious problems getting his hair to spike the Bowie way."

For a time the two lived at the flat of their friend Linda Ashby, a lesbian prostitute whose flashy West End brothel acted as a squat for various members of Sid and John's circle of friends, friends who would ultimately become the inner circle of Sex Pistols' fans and followers.

Life on their side of the tracks was not easy. As they drifted amid the teenage wasteland of central London, they were easy prey to hucksters, hipsters and anarchists seeking impressionable young minds to mould.

* * *

Whatever else he might have been or thought, Malcolm Robert Andrew McLaren had certainly considered anarchism as a way forward. In 1971 Malcolm opened a clothes shop called Let It Rock at 430 King's Road. The name of the shop had changed a few times over the years but it was located not too far from the rehearsal room where the band run by Steve Jones gathered to make their noise. It still included Paul Cook and Wally Nightingale but the bassist, Del

Sid, aged 17.

Let It Rock was hardly run of the mill. Malcolm, in keeping with his contrary nature, took delight in ignoring current trends and instead concentrated on Teddy Boy and fifties fashions, drape jackets and brothel creeper shoes, skinny ties and drainpipe trousers. Malcolm's girlfriend, fashion designer Vivienne Westwood, was a partner in the enterprise and she was wont to try out any new ideas she had in the shop. Six months after opening Malcolm changed the name of the shop to Too Fast To Live, Too Young To Die.

It was inevitable that a shop with a name like that would attract teenagers and eventually Steve, Paul and Wally started to hang around the place. Malcolm got wind of the fact that they were 'a band', heard the tinkle of cash registers, and got them a proper place to rehearse in Covent Garden. The group, however, were less than enthusiastic, they didn't like Covent Garden and besides they still had no bass guitarist.

Malcolm McLaren's 'Saturday boy' was a young man called Glen Matlock who by a strange coincidence was also a fan of The Small Faces, and by an even stranger coincidence owned and played a bass guitar extremely well. Glen and Steve got into conversation one Saturday morning in the shop and as a result Glen was invited to audition for the group. Glen, in fact, played along to The Faces' number 'Three Button Hand-Me-Down' in Wally's bedroom and so, at long last, the band had recruited what seemed like a permanent bass guitarist.

The group got definite 'bad vibes' from the Covent Garden rehearsal room and so moved on to 90 Lots Road SW10, a place found by Steve Jones. Warwick Nightingale's father was the boss of a firm of electricians who had been contracted to rewire the BBC's latest acquisition, Riverside Studios, close to Hammersmith Bridge. The group used Mr Nightingale Senior's keys, had a duplicate set cut and moved into what had been the old sound dubbing room.

The acoustics of this room, purported to be the best in Europe, and its generous size allowed the group free rein to expand both their versatility as writers and their prowess as instrumentalists. Two original songs emerged, 'Scarface' written by Wally and 'Did You No Wrong', the eventual B-side of 'God Save The Queen' written by Glen. It seems quite extraordinary that a noisy rock group could

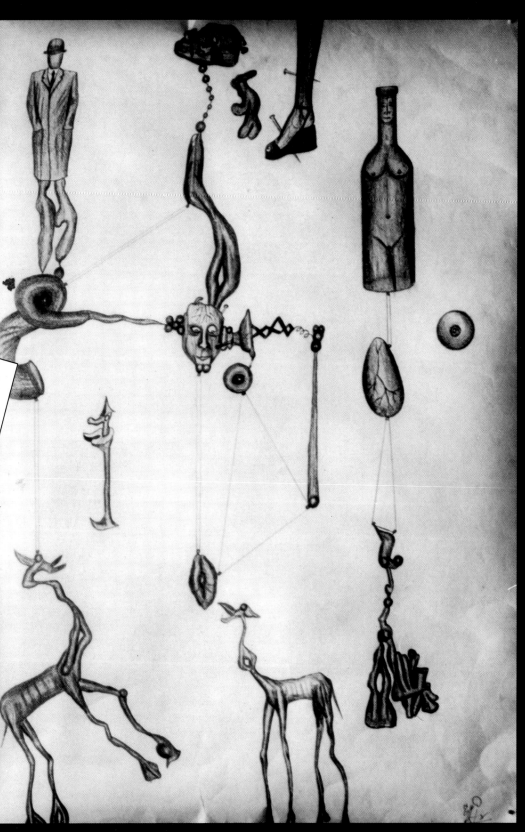

Sid's figurative drawing from 1974.

rehearse in a BBC sound room, coming and going as they pleased for 12 months without being challenged, but unlikely as it may seem this is how the fledgling Sex Pistols, with their stolen equipment, learned how to become a group.

At last the group had a name. They'd been calling themselves The Swankers but Malcolm McLaren, by this time a regular visitor at rehearsals, had other ideas. He was becoming more and more involved not only in the music of the group but also their personal lives.

Amongst the names he had in mind were The Q.T. Sex Pistols. He even had T-shirts printed bearing the logo 'Kutie Jones and His Sex Pistols' which were sold in his shop. By this time the shop had undergone another name change: now it was called Sex.

The group had other ideas for names, however: Kid Gladlove and The Strand – after the Roxy Music Song – were just two of them.

The band had yet to play a live show but this changed in early 1975 when they played a one-off gig at a private party thrown in the flat above Tom Slater's Café at 205 King's Road. This show, if three numbers actually constitute a show, was given by an unnamed band who performed 'I'm A Road Runner', the sixties classic originally recorded by Junior Walker And The All Stars, 'Watcha Gonna Do About It?' by The Small Faces and their original song 'Scarface'.

Around this time Malcolm had moved to the USA and had talked his way into becoming the manager of The New York Dolls. Media favourites who lacked any serious commercial base, The Dolls were the next best thing to a US equivalent of a glam rock outfit: all make-up and hair, raucous raunchy music much derived from The Rolling Stones circa 1972, and a deviant lifestyle that suggested every form of decadence known to man. Their image had been etched into stone when, on their first visit to the UK in 1972, drummer Billy Murcia died from an overdose of pills and alcohol.

The Dolls were led by singer David Johansen, whose rubbery lips were as voluptuous as those of his hero Mick Jagger, and their chief instrumentalist was guitarist Johnny Thunders, a fireball with spiked black hair that actually pre-empted the look that Keith Richards would adopt when Ron Wood became his sidekick.

Right: **Press cutting from May 1974.**

Opposite: **Pen sketch of Sid by a friend of Anne Beverley, early 1976.**

WAS HACKNEY STUDENT DRUGGED AT PARTY?

Malcolm's tenure as their manager didn't last beyond an aborted attempt to dress them all in red costumes and promote them as a Communist conspiracy beneath a hammer and sickle backdrop. Within six months Malcolm was on his way back to the UK and with him came a recently acquired white Gibson Les Paul guitar probably, once, the property of Sylvain Sylvain of The Dolls. It was the guitar that Steve Jones used for most of The Pistols' career.

Although Malcolm's venture into the world of rock 'n' roll management had been fairly short-lived, he had well and truly been bitten by the entrepreneurial bug, so much so that on his return he put forward the idea of managing the group who had, at this point, more or less gone along with the idea of being called The Sex Pistols. His shop became their command centre. There was, however, one major obstacle standing in the way of any future development. Wally would have to go.

Warwick Nightingale had formed the group; due to his father's – and the BBC's – lack of security the group had found a place to rehearse; he had been the spur to egg on the rest when they had been quite content to hang around swigging lager.

But his face didn't fit, he didn't look the part, and with typical McLaren buck passing it fell to Steve Jones to dismiss Wally. This he did swiftly and painlessly at the band's next rehearsal before assuming the role of lead guitarist himself.

John Tiberi, who would become The Sex Pistols' principal road manager and assume the name of Boogie, recollects: "This was a guy who couldn't read, well he could barely write; he put his mind to it that he was going to play guitar and nothing was going to stop him. And he got bloody good at it. I've heard him play classical on acoustic and he's great."

This still left Malcolm with the vexed question of who was to replace Steve as lead singer and front man. He had set his sights on various American singers including Richard Hell of Television or Johnny Thunders, the rooster-haired guitarist with The New York Dolls, but the group insisted that their lead singer should be British and the same age as they were.

Glen was friendly with Midge Ure, at that time lead singer with Slik, and he had a word with him about the possibility of joining The Pistols but he appeared to be uninterested.

Apart from being the centre of action for The Pistols, Sex was doing

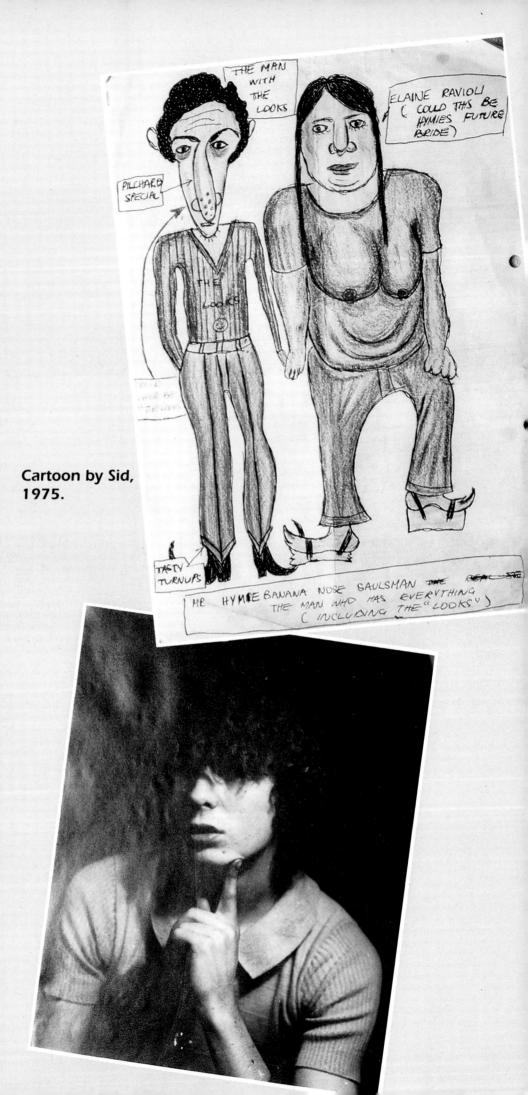

Cartoon by Sid, 1975.

26

very nicely not only with the Teddy Boy fashions but also with a variety of rubber and leather fetish clothing, much of it decorated with bondage straps. Alongside these were the futuristic and outrageous fashion designs of Vivienne Westwood's colourful garments.

Anne Beverley recalls: "You wouldn't believe this, but they had macs with no sleeves, what damn good are they to anyone?"

John and Sid had, by this time, also discovered King's Road and between the pair of them had got to know the in-places very well and on a Saturday afternoon in August 1975 John Lydon walked into the shop called Sex. He certainly wasn't difficult to spot at the time: in addition to his green hair John had become the proud owner of a ripped-up jacket loosely held together by safety pins.

During the next few weeks John spent a long time chatting to Steve, Paul and Glen who by this time were all doing part time work in the shop. They told him about the group and their ideas for music and it was finally agreed that an audition would be set up at the Roebuck Inn at 354 King's Road.

There are two versions of the audition of John Lydon. It is anybody's guess whether Lydon auditioned in the Roebuck miming to Alice Cooper's 'School's Out' on the juke box or whether it took place in McLaren's clothes shop and that the record was Cooper's 'Eighteen'. Wherever it was held, or whatever the record, both the group and McLaren liked him so much that he was taken on as lead singer and front man without delay.

Thus came about the creation of The Sex Pistols, the band that in time would make and break Sid Vicious.

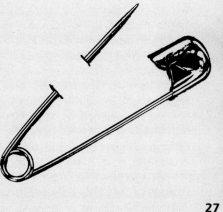

3

From Simon to Sid, birth of The Pistols and Sid the punk

"It's rotten, is that! You're rotten, you are! Yes, you, you're rotten!"

Like many a teenager before him and like many after, John Lydon latched on to a saying so much so that it was used to the point of boredom.

Glen Matlock: "He used the word rotten all the blasted time, everything was rotten. Not just, how are you feeling? Rotten! but every damn thing. So I christened him Rotten, and it stuck."

The King's Road, the stomping ground of The Sex Pistols, had by this time become the fashion centre of England yet again. Shops were opening everywhere, all hoping to cash in on the latest fad. Malcolm McLaren openly welcomed the competition; imitation, he decided, was the sincerest form of flattery.

One such rival shop was a store known as Acme Attractions, and the staff of Sex noted with some satisfaction that whatever Malcolm did today, Acme did six months later. Among the retail staff at Acme were Don Letts, who would later become a member of Big Audio Dynamite and, on a casual basis, Sid Vicious.

The Sex Pistols Mark 1: Johnny Rotten, Glen Matlock, Steve Jones and Paul Cook.

Bernie Rhodes, soon to become the manager of The Clash, walked into Sex one morning with a very strange tale about Acme. Glen Matlock: "Bernie wandered into our shop grinning all over his face, he said, 'I don't believe that Sid. A woman's just walked into the shop with something that apparently didn't work and demanded either an exchange or a refund. Quick as a flash, Sid drops his pants and says, 'If it don't work get some of this'."

It was clear to everyone, not least John Lydon and Malcolm McLaren, that this kind of behaviour was ideally suited to being a Sex Pistol. But there were no vacancies at the present time.

Though Lydon was preoccupied with the group, he and Sid remained fast friends, John leading with Sid following lemming-like behind. Sid was jealous of John's leading role in The Pistols, and was more than a tad incredulous that someone as seemingly aimless as John Lydon could front a rock band. To see for himself he went along with John to watch the band play at Ravensbourne College of Art in Chislehurst on December 12, 1975.

Sid loved the sound, the ideas, the music; he thought The Pistols were great and wanted to dance. The trouble was Sid couldn't dance, so instead he began jumping up and down, his legs and arms flailing all over the place, in his version of how he thought teenagers ought to be reacting to the music of The Pistols. He looked just like a pogo-stick, the children's toy which utilises a spring loaded pole for vigorous up and down movement. Thus was born the pogo, the universal punk dance which Sid has rightly been credited with inventing. Within 12 months every self-respecting punk in England would be dancing the pogo to their favourite punk band.

Once The Pistols had established themselves and broken the ice, clones started to arrive on the scene and, fanned by a rock press starved of something new to write about, punk took off. To Sid, David Bowie had, overnight, become passé, boring, out of touch. Punk rock was the new, vibrant thing.

There appeared on the scene the 'Bromley Contingent' whose most notable alumni were Billy Idol, born William Broad and soon to lead Generation X, and Siouxsie Sioux, born Janet Susan Ballion and given to wearing fishnet stockings, swastikas and black peep-hole bras which 29 displayed her nipples. Others included Steven Bailey, later Steve Havoc and later still Steve Severin; Sue Lucas, the original Sue Catwoman; Debbie Wilson, also known as Debbie Juvenile; and Tracey O'Keefe who died at the age of 19, one of the first casualties of punk, and whose coffin bore a wreath from Malcolm McLaren decorated with the word 'bollocks' in red flowers. Suddenly it seemed that anyone could join a punk band.

The centre of punk activity was the 100 Club, at 100 Oxford Street, which in former days had been a successful jazz cellar. The Sex Pistols secured a Tuesday night residency during the summer of 1976 and Sid was always prominent among the group of die-hard fans who crowded towards the stage during their sets. It was on such a night as this that Nick Kent, writer of distinction for New Musical Express, had the misfortune to block Sid's view of the stage. Sid, aware that he needed to prove his status amongst his peers, took a length of bicycle chain from around his waist and struck Kent over the head with a mighty blow.

The legend was beginning to grow.

Ron Watts, the proprietor of the 100 Club, was not slow to notice the crowds that punk drew into his club, and together with McLaren he conceived the idea of the 100 Club Punk Festival to take place in September of that year. The bill for the first concert included The Sex Pistols, now far and away the leaders of the pack, The Clash, not far behind, The Subway Sect, who never achieved much, and Siouxsie And The Banshees, the group formed by Siouxsie Sioux and Steve Bailey (now Havoc) on the spur of the moment. The Banshees line-up was augmented by guitarist Marco Pironi, who'd also played with Chelsea, and Sid on drums.

"It was meant to be our 15 minutes of fame," Siouxsie said later. "But we managed to sustain it for 10 years, which only goes to show how addictive dressing up and making a noise for a living can be."

The début appearance of The Banshees did not get off to a very auspicious start. They had come to an arrangement with The Clash to share their amplifiers. Groups are always sensitive about sharing equipment, especially drummers, but on this occasion it had been agreed, for once and for the sake of 'punk' unity, to relax the kind of territorial guarding usually reserved for more sensitive musicians.

However, all the sweet talk and creeping that had enabled The Banshees to use this gear almost came to nothing because Sid and Siouxsie, in a gesture best remembered as tactless in the extreme even by Sid's standards, had chosen this gig to wear swastikas as part of their stage wear. Jewish Bernie Rhodes, prowling the arena as manager of The Clash, not unnaturally took exception.

After a few well-chosen phrases had been exchanged between Sid and Bernie, The Banshees finally played a short set which consisted of a 20-minute medley of 'The Lord's Prayer', 'Twist And Shout', and 'Knocking On Heaven's Door'. The consensus of opinion amongst those watching The Banshees that night was that they were terrible. Some observers feel that this exposure with The Banshees helped make Sid Vicious a star but his mother correctly insists that Sid was famous on the punk scene long before he even joined a band.

This notoriety was further enhanced on the second night of the 100 Club Punk Festival when The Buzzcocks from Manchester, The Vibrators, including for this performance Chris Spedding on guitar, The Damned and French band The Stinky Toys performed. It was during the interval between The Vibrators and The Damned that a glass was thrown from the audience which smashed against one of the pillars close to the stage. A shard of glass ricochetted from the pillar, struck a young girl and blinded her in one eye.

Vivienne Westwood was one of those present who saw Sid throw the glass but she has subsequently admitted lying to the police by protesting Sid's innocence. However, Sid was arrested and taken to a remand home for young offenders. Sid knew full well he was the guilty party but somehow he managed to convince himself he was innocent.

The following day the newspapers had a field day denouncing punk rock and its followers. Ron Watts decided to ban all future punk gigs at his club.

What is indisputable is that after this excursion into drumming for The Banshees Sid hung up his drumsticks and left. He went from there to one of the most famous non-bands of the punk age. Formed out of boredom with squat life, The Flowers Of Romance never played a single live show but had countless rehearsals at The Clash's studio and at various squats around London.

Their style was brash, loud and fast, very much in the style of The

Above: **Sid, Steve Bailey and Siouxsie Sioux at London's 100 Club.**

Below: **Sid with Paul Cook.**

Above: **Glen Matlock, wearing a McLaren/Westwood design shirt.** Left: **Johnny Rotten.**

Above: **Matlock and Rotten.**

Right: **Sid flies to Sweden.**

carte blanche **to ban anything even loosely contentious. Meanwhile their record 'Anarchy In The UK' sold like hot cakes.**

In a few short months The Sex Pistols had come from nowhere to being the best known, and certainly most notorious, rock group in Britain.

* * *

The Pistols' UK tour was to have featured three other bands, The Clash, The Damned and, from New York, The Heartbreakers, lately assembled by guitarist Johnny Thunders from the ashes of The New York Dolls. Arriving in London with them was Nancy Anne Spungen.

Nancy was from a well-to-do American Jewish family from Philadelphia. Clearly the black sheep of the family, as soon as she was old enough to go her own way she left home and headed for New York where she became part of the alternative rock scene that developed around CBGBs and Max's Kansas City. She hung out with The New York Dolls, formed a liaison with their drummer Jerry Nolan, took heroin and became known as a fairly desperate groupie, an unabashed name dropper and one of life's born losers.

Her relationship with Nolan over, Nancy had hoped to latch on to Johnny Thunders but he showed no interest. Nevertheless she followed Thunders and his Heartbreakers over to London, already aware that the punk scene in London was thriving.

The idea of still-swinging England and the reputation of such groups as The Clash, The Damned and The Sex Pistols attracted her enormously. It is likely that she thought that whatever mess her personal life was in, it would be easier to clean up and come to terms with in a different location. She was already experiencing the first symptoms of heroin dependency.

Since time immemorial there has existed an underground grapevine in London and other major cities that unites junkies, a mental 'chat line' for those dependent on heroin for their daily existence. When Nancy arrived in London, she was quick to pick up on this and made her way to the King's Road to experience first hand the 'punk' lifestyle.

The obvious place to set up base was in one of the many squats around the King's Road area. With her bleached hair and torn clothing, she looked the picture of punkdom and it didn't take long for her to be accepted as one of them. Her problem

Cook and Jones.

was that she was her own worst enemy: she never stopped talking and, as if that wasn't enough, she had the knack of forgetting to engage her brain before opening her mouth. As a result she upset most of the people most of the time.

"Everybody would pick on her," remembers Anne Beverley. "Some people ignored her but Sid felt sorry for her, you know, he wanted to help her. That's how it all started and once they'd got together that was it."

John and Sid were now sharing a flat that doubled as a brothel whose other occupants were lesbian prostitutes. Somehow Nancy found her way there. Initially she made a play for the great Johnny Rotten, but the most notorious Sex Pistol was actually rather puritanical about girls who threw themselves at him so he passed her on to his best pal Sid.

It is likely that Nancy deeply wished that her Sid would become a more integral member of The Pistols rather than just a deeply committed fan. Either way she pressurised him to become a punk musician, preferably a Pistol, and this probably played a major part in what later became known as the Glen Matlock Affair.

* * *

Malcolm McLaren, meanwhile, was wallowing in the furore created by both the EMI and Bill Grundy episodes. He also discovered what he perceived as a deadly secret about Glen Matlock: he liked The Beatles. In the court of King Malcolm this was treason.

Although this was the official reason given for Glen Matlock's surprising and abrupt departure from The Pistols, the true reasons were somewhat more complex.

Glen was rapidly becoming the outsider in the group. He certainly didn't share the extrovert character of Johnny Rotten, neither was he a sneering ne'er-do-well like Steve Jones or a passive misfit like his sidekick Paul Cook, both of whom were happy to drink and screw their way around London. Johnny Rotten now had his own entourage, prominent amongst them being Sid Vicious, and Matlock was off limits.

While Matlock could hardly be described as sensitive, he was certainly cut from a different cloth from that of his colleagues. For starters he was a genuine musician, the only real musician in the band, with an ear for harmonies and arrangements and a knack of composing which the others 3 lacked, though in this department Jones was rapidly catching up.

Professionally, things had started to go wrong at the group's first 100 Club gig where John's drunkenness did not sit well with the ever professional Matlock. A slanging match developed between songs, and though the genuine anger on-stage actually contributed to the atmosphere of the performance, when Rotten shouted 'I'll kill you" at Matlock, he probably meant it.

Malcolm McLaren, of course, lapped it up and he also admired the couldn't-care-less attitudes of Steve and Paul. So when Matlock let slip in an unguarded moment that he actually admired The Beatles, the writing was on the wall.

On February 28, 1977, Derek Johnson, news editor of the New Musical Express was sent the following telegram: 'Derek; Yes, Glen Matlock was thrown out of The Sex Pistols because he went on too long about Paul McCartney, stop. EMI was enough, stop. The Beatles were too much, stop. Sid Vicious, their best friend and always a member of the group but as yet unheard has been enlisted, stop. His best credential is that he gave Nick Kent what he deserved many months ago at the 100 Club, stop. Love and Peace, stop. Malcolm McLaren.'

Sounds magazine covered the story on March 5, 1977: 'Pistols sack bassist, Matlock, for liking McCartney!!'

Glen Matlock, the only true musician amongst them, and the one who would continue to write songs for them, was sacked and therefore officially unemployed for daring to like one of the best writer-musicians of this century.

This unemployment was to be short-lived however, as Glen reappeared shortly afterwards with his new group, The Rich Kids, signed with undue haste by EMI, doubtless because they were aware of his musical capabilities.

Sid Vicious was a Sex Pistol at last.

Sid joins The Pistols.

The very name Sex Pistols – Sid joins The Pistols

Glen Matlock's final performance as the bass player for The Sex Pistols took place at a sell-out concert on the stage of the Paradiso Club in Amsterdam on January 7, 1977. The music press back home in England, even if they'd had an inkling as to what was going to happen, did not announce his departure from the group until March.

McLaren and The Pistols had actually auditioned Sid Vicious for the position of bassist on February 11 at the group's rehearsal room near the old Tin Pan Alley Club at 6 Denmark Street. Since Sid had little or no knowledge of the rudiments of bass guitar playing he passed his audition with flying colours.

Sid, therefore, was set to join the most notorious band in the world. It didn't seem to matter to him that the future prospects of the band were not at all healthy at that time.

Their recording contract with EMI had been terminated, and regardless of McLaren's later statements, it was not through mutual consent. It must surely have been the first time in the history of EMI that an artist had been dumped after a début smash hit. The 39 contract was terminated on January 22.

Glen Matlock had been one of the deciding factors in the initial signing of The Pistols to EMI. John Darnley, former EMI A&R man who was with the company at the time of The Pistols, knew full well that without Matlock The Pistols days as a musical entity – as opposed to a punk icon – were virtually numbered. "The whole point was that we knew that Glen was the only musician amongst them," he says. "It's obvious we felt very strongly about his removal from the group, a bit like firing John Lennon or Paul McCartney from The Beatles. What with that and all the adverse publicity we felt we were better off without him. As I said, Glen was the musician and when he got together with Midge Ure, Steve New and Rusty Egan as The Rich Kids we signed them straight away."

Due to the unprecedented press interest and furore resulting from their outbursts on the Bill Grundy show, their credibility with all but a handful of radical promoters had plummeted to zero. Agents and theatre managers did not book acts who were as unpredictable as The Pistols had become. Far better to book a lesser known but probably more reliable band who would do the gig, please the kids and leave without upsetting anyone.

Sid, however, had been in love with the idea of being a Sex Pistol, ever since he had seen the success that John Lydon, his college friend and accomplice, enjoyed. He also knew that whatever EMI and the rock promoters felt, the punks themselves, the fans, were firmly on the side of The Pistols. The offer was made and Sid readily accepted on February 18, 1977.

Matlock doesn't seem to have been too concerned that his role in the leading punk band was over – that would come later, when the money was being counted – and in a genuine gesture of punk unity he even offered to teach Sid how to play. "I told him there were no sour grapes and that I'd give him lessons to get his playing up to standard and he said that he'd give me a call when he needed me. He obviously thought that he didn't because I never got that call."

Some performers have such a natural affinity with their instruments that sheer determination gets them through and Sid, it must be said, took to bass guitar like a duck to water. He would never be a virtuoso but he was 40 certainly adequate, and since the

music of The Pistols was at best basic, Sid's hell for leather enthusiasm was sufficient to propel The Pistols in the bass department. Even now, when a bass guitarist plays in a fundamental and fast driving style, the remark that is most often passed is that the player is an exponent of the 'Sid Vicious style of bass playing'.

Whether or not the speed at which his hands moved on the bass was related to the accuracy of his fretting or was intended to bludgeon the listeners into a false sense of security is debatable, but at this and most other stages in The Pistols' career, the image was as important as the music.

With EMI now out of the picture, McLaren was exploring several avenues to bring about another, hopefully longer lasting, contract not only to give The Sex Pistols more credibility but also to feather his own nest.

He could probably have signed with any number of companies because, as many a shrewd manager has realised, notoriety is preferable to obscurity and breeds interest which in turn breeds demand and therefore money.

CBS Records appeared to be very interested. They'd read all about punk rock and in common with other companies wanted a slice of the action. So did Chrysalis and Polydor. McLaren, to his credit, spent practically the whole of February in meeting after meeting with the powers that be at CBS. But once again discretion prevailed. CBS, more than a little worried by The Pistols' reputation, decided on a much safer bet, The Clash. Compared with The Sex Pistols The Clash were pussycats when it came to outrage, but at least The Clash could play their instruments with some degree of competence.

Early in March The Pistols, anxious to do something, booked into Wessex recording studios and enlisted the services of Chris Thomas as producer. Thomas was a freelance record producer who had initially been involved when the group were at EMI.

"Mike Thorne at EMI had put Malcolm McLaren in touch with Chris Thomas to produce 'Anarchy' and the result was great," says John Darnley. "But when they got rid of Glen, we lost interest. However Chris Thomas remained as the group's producer right up to the time of Dave Goodman."

Due to Sid's inexperience and temporary inadequacy on bass, Steve Jones laid down bass on the backing tracks and then overdubbed lead gui-

tar afterwards. At least The Pistols played on their own records. However, any bass figures put down on this particular session were quickly learned by Sid who was becoming more and more confident as each week passed.

This confidence had much to do with the support of John who had rightly figured that with Sid in the ranks he had at least one loyal supporter in any decisions that had to be made. John now knew that his vote counted 50 per cent, not 25 per cent, since where he went Sid would surely follow. Additionally, Sid would do almost anything to help fuel the publicity machine, a factor which McLaren, at least, appreciated.

As for Sid, he didn't care about anything or anyone and if he couldn't find a fight to join he'd simply start one with whoever was in the vicinity. If Malcolm had suggested jumping into the Thames he'd have done so, provided John gave him the nod first.

Sid's first public appearance as a Sex Pistol was not on-stage but for a photo call outside Buckingham Palace at a public 'signing' with their next label, A&M Records. After considerable negotiation with A&M a contract that was mutually acceptable to both parties was drawn up. This guaranteed to pay the group £150,000 over a two-year period, with an initial advance of £50,000, provided that they presented the record company with a minimum of 18 songs per year. That works out at £4166 per song in addition to any royalties that might arise.

The contract was signed on March 9, 1977, and with A&M anxiously awaiting the first single McLaren and the group decided to present them with an existing track, already recorded, originally titled 'No Future' but retitled 'God Save The Queen'. This was to be the first single for their new record company.

On the same day A&M threw a party for The Pistols at their offices. John drank like a fish and insulted everyone in sight, Steve had his way with a secretary in a toilet and Sid set about the plumbing in a second loo.

A&M were not pleased but both parties turned up the following day outside Buckingham Palace. The group revelled in this unforeseen publicity stunt and arrived in a black Daimler limousine still not sober from the previous day's revelries. They fell

out onto the pavement and carried out the fake signing, laughed and joked with the press, gave them the inevitable 'two fingered' salute, piled back into their Daimler and were gone. Sid distinguished himself by suggesting to a female reporter from the Daily Express that the previous week he'd seen her... 'at a party stuck on so and so's cock.'

The day after this little charade Johnny Rotten appeared in court charged with possessing drugs, namely, speed. He was found guilty and fined £40.

That evening The Pistols visited The Speakeasy, a well known club near Oxford Circus much frequented by music industry types. While they were there a scuffle broke out and Radio One DJ 'Whispering' Bob Harris was slightly injured. Whilst The Pistols were only marginally involved, they were held responsible; indeed, The Pistols were on the point of being held responsible for any outbreak of violence that might have taken place within 10 miles of the West End.

The new single 'God Save The Queen', having been duly delivered to A&M Records, was pressed and issued in plain brown A&M sleeves. Only a limited number of these records ever 'escaped' because the company was beginning to have second thoughts about its new, rather impulsive signing. The behaviour of the group, the incidents at their offices, the so-called signing outside Buckingham Palace, Johnny Rotten's court appearance and the subsequent fracas at the Speakeasy had left a nasty taste in the mouths of A&M executives. McLaren was summoned to the offices of A&M for a meeting on the morning of March 16 and as a result of McLaren's refusal to accept any criticism of his group and A&M's entrenched position regarding standards of behaviour, the contract between the two parties was terminated.

A&M had, in fact, decided to cut their losses; the original £50,000 advance against the contracted £150,000 stayed in the group's hands and in addition they handed McLaren a cheque for £25,000 as compensation for losing the contract. That's a total of £75,000 for a week's non-work: £10,715 per day or £100 per hour per group member.

"They've given us up through fear and business pressure," Rotten told the press. "They've kicked us in the teeth. We mean what we say. A record company is there to market records not dictate."

PISTOLS

After only one week the group were again without a recording contract. At this stage many a manager would have given up, but not Malcolm McLaren. It was decided to fly the group to Jersey for what should have been an idyllic, get-away-from-it-all holiday. They arrived in Jersey on March 22 and returned to England on the 23rd having been ordered off the island.

"When we got to Jersey the Customs bloke wanted to search my arse so I farted in his face," was Sid's sole comment on the brief Channel island sojourn.

They were then packed off to Berlin where they were photographed alongside the Berlin Wall on Malcolm's instructions. They arrived home at the end of March and within days Sid was admitted to hospital with hepatitis. The doctors put this down to misuse of drugs.

It is not clear exactly when Sid started using heroin but it seems likely that it began around the time of the Berlin trip which was within weeks of his meeting Nancy Spungen and joining The Pistols.

McLaren now set about the task of finding a third label for the group and, as a last resort, approached Virgin, the empire founded by bearded Richard Branson whose hippy-like demeanour was the very antithesis of all that McLaren stood for. Accompanied by his lawyer, Stephen Fisher, he met with Branson and a deal was struck. Within four days Malcolm not only managed to tie up the Virgin deal but also a deal with Barclay Records in Paris to cover France, Switzerland, Zanzibar and Algeria for an advance of £26,000.

The contract with Virgin was signed on Friday, May 13. John, Steve and Paul signed first and the group as a whole was advanced £15,000. Sid signed three days later on his discharge from hospital.

The first task that fell to Virgin Records was to salvage 'God Save The Queen'. Designer Jamie Reid was involved by this time and had come up with some inspired artwork which involved adding a number of embellishments to the official Daily Express portrait of the Queen specially commissioned for the Silver Jubilee. This was to be the picture sleeve for 'God Save The Queen' b/w 'Did You No Wrong'.

Independent labels, of which Virgin was one, usually managed to do deals with major record companies involving the use of their pressing plants. The CBS plant at Aylesbury 47 pressed Virgin's records and was now expected to press The Sex Pistols' single. After initially refusing to press the record due to an unprecedented walk out by staff (unprecedented at CBS anyway), a compromise was reached. Elsewhere in the city, platemakers refused to cut plates for the sleeve as it involved unflattering alterations to the Queen's portrait. Yet again this was resolved and the record finally went on sale on May 27.

Malcolm McLaren's troubles were by no means over. The BBC, to no-one's surprise, promptly banned the record from its TV and radio stations, a gesture virtually guaranteed to ensure that it would be a hit. Woolworth and W.H. Smith immediately followed suit by banning it from their stores. Several other national chains also refused to stock the single. Despite this, the record clocked up sales of 150,000 in the first five days via various independent outlets. With sales like that the record was clearly heading for the number one spot but, according to the Gallup Chart, it never rose higher than number two. This was obviously to save the BBC's face as they were more or less obliged to play the number one record on Top Of The Pops.

On June 7, The Pistols decided to throw their own Jubilee Party on board the aptly named Queen Elizabeth river boat. The idea was simplicity itself, board the ship at London Bridge, sail up to Hammersmith, turn round and re-dock at Westminster Bridge.

"It was going to be a fun day, or rather evening," says Anne Beverley. "We had to be there at 5.30 p.m. There was this smashing boat with tables full of food and there was plenty to drink as well. The boys were going to play during the course of the evening, you know, just a good party. Once the band members, numerous friends and hangers-on and of course the press gang were on board we set sail. By the time we got level with the Houses of Parliament the party was in full swing and the band were performing 'Anarchy In The UK'. I felt very sorry for Jah Wobble, he just wanted a good laugh like the rest of us but this French photographer kept hassling him for pictures, kept pushing it all the time so Wobble knocked his camera out of his hand."

The captain of the ship, a stickler for discipline, observed these happenings and decided to take no chances on the party getting out of hand and called in the River Police.

48   The result was that an Armada of

boats came ploughing down the Thames. The party was stopped and as the ship docked a bevy of baton-wielding police rushed on board and made several arrests.

Among those charged were McLaren (using insulting words likely to cause a breach of the peace) who was later released on £100 bail; Vivi-enne Westwood (obstructing the police); Jamie Reid (assault); and John Lydon (assault) who was fined £3 after pleading guilty. Somehow Sid avoided being snatched.

The following day Virgin Records, not so easily shaken as EMI or A&M, signed the band to a European deal worth £75,000. By June 10, the group's Jubilee single had topped sales of 200,000. All that in just two weeks.

But persistently preaching anarchy and debunking royalty is likely to result in someone, somewhere, taking grave exception and so it was with The Sex Pistols. The first attack on the band and entourage occurred on June 13 when Jamie Reid was set upon by a gang of youths and suf-fered a broken nose and broken leg. Five days later Johnny Rotten, pro-ducer Chris Thomas and engineer Bill Price were attacked by a gang of razor-swinging thugs and both Rotten and Thomas required stitches.

On June 19 Paul Cook was attacked by a gang carrying iron bars as he left Shepherds Bush tube sta-tion. The result was 15 stitches in the back of his head.

"That was a bad time all round for the boys," says Dave Goodman, their sound engineer. "They would travel around together in cabs. I remember Sid and John turning up absolutely petrified. Sid hated the name Vicious, especially at this time because he just wasn't! The guy was skinny, you know... 26-inch waist and quite hon-estly he couldn't have struck terror into anybody!"

5

Sid, Nancy and the split

In the early part of July, Virgin Records, anxious to cash in on their success with 'God Save The Queen', issued The Sex Pistols' second single, 'Pretty Vacant'. Compared to its predecessor, it was a fairly innocuous number which was guaranteed not to offend anyone but all the same it was banned by the twin powers of Woolworth and W.H. Smith just for being a Sex Pistols record.

Jamie Reid bought the picture frame featured on the cover from an antique shop. "It was just the right size, seven inches by seven, so I smashed it myself, to get the right effect, while I was walking up the street." This was also the first record for which the band had produced a promotional video.

By this time Sid and Nancy Spungen were living in a flat in Chelsea Cloisters. "Si called it Chelsea Closets on account of the fact that it was like a monk's cell," says Anne Beverley. "It was really old fashioned... a bit like the flat we had in Drury Lane with just as many mod cons. It had what Si called a bloody high level grill, I think he used to have to stand on a chair to do his toast."

On July 7 Nancy appeared in court charged with carrying an offensive weapon, a truncheon, in her handbag. The judge was lenient with her when he discovered the sort of attacks that had been carried out on The Pistols. She could have been deported but the judge decided not to send her back to the USA, especially when she told him that she fully

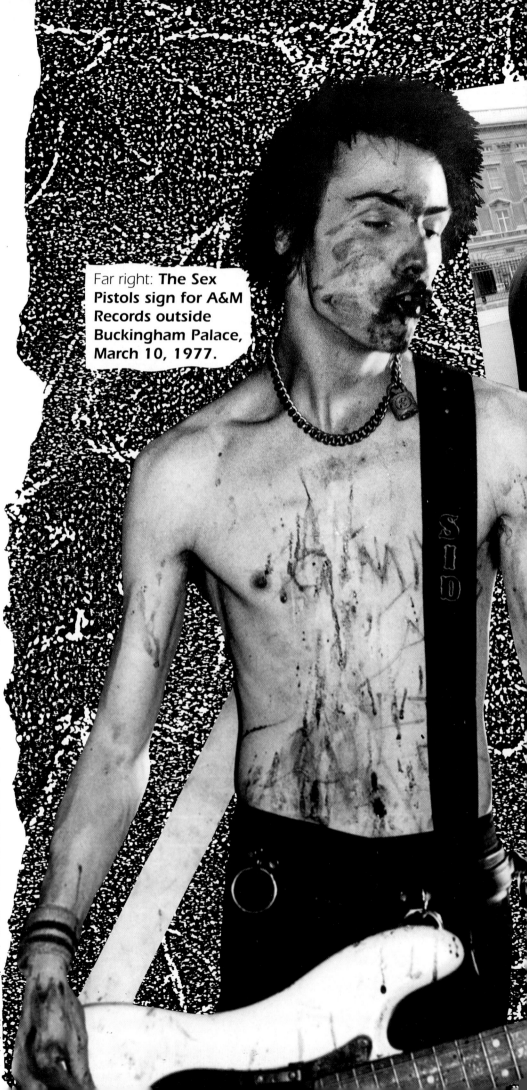

Far right: **The Sex Pistols sign for A&M Records outside Buckingham Palace, March 10, 1977.**

intended to marry Sid Vicious.

Shortly afterwards The Pistols left for a tour of Scandinavia lasting two weeks, finishing on July 28, and while they were away the BBC had a change of heart about The Sex Pistols. They hadn't banned 'Pretty Vacant', and the video was shown on Top Of The Pops on July 14. The record reached number seven in the BBC/Gallup Top 100.

Sid, unfortunately, had to interrupt the Scandinavian tour to return home to appear in Court to answer charges arising from a punch up at the 100 Club Punk Festival in 1976. He had been on bail for a year. Charged with being in illegal possession of a flick knife, he attended court in a black suit and tie with his characteristic spiked hair flattened down specially for the occasion. Appearing for his defence and as character witnesses were Clash members Paul Simenon and Mick Jones, along with journalist Caroline Coon who'd covered the punk scene in detail for Melody Maker and who was a veteran of court procedure having for many years been involved with Release, the organisation formed to counsel drug offenders.

"Mick Jones was a real mate to Sid," says Anne Beverley. "He was always there for him, and Caroline Coon. She was the star of the trial. They were trying to set him up, just because he had a flick knife in his pocket. She wouldn't have any of it."

The outcome of the trial couldn't have suited Sid, his mother, the entourage or Virgin Records better. The Judge was not one of those "er... what is a punk rocker?" types; on the contrary he appeared to have a bias towards punk rock in general and The Sex Pistols in particular. He gave Sid a stern reprimand and fined him £125.

The same day, as the result of a bet, Sid and Caroline Coon took tea in the elegant surroundings of Harrods restaurant. Sid was still wearing the suit and tie, perhaps just as well.

He rejoined the Scandinavian tour for the last few days and the whole group arrived back on July 30. England, however, was not as hospitable to The Pistols as Scandinavia.

During their absence their status as Public Enemy Number One had resulted in bans on live work that stretched from Land's End to John O'Groats. There was nowhere that they could obtain bookings for live gigs.

Malcolm McLaren was philosophical about the situation, albeit concerned about the steady influx of money drying up. So he decided to put the band out on the road on a secret undercover tour. Crucial to the scheme was his decision to hold back announcements of the shows until the day before or even the day of the show itself. Unfortunately, no matter how little advance warning was given, sooner or later the name Sex Pistols would rear its ugly head. To get around this problem various alternative names were thought up.

The Spots – (S)ex (P)istols (O)n (T)our (S)ecretly – was the name used most often and was also the most successful. Other names used were The Tax Exiles and The Hamsters. The tour, which again was very successful, took up the best part of August and the first 10 days or so of September.

Sid and Nancy now moved out of Chelsea 'Closets' and found a better flat in Maida Vale. The lease on the property only ran for seven years and when Malcolm was made aware of this limitation, his reaction was: "That's OK, he'll be dead by then anyway."

The next Sex Pistols single was 'Holidays In The Sun'. This produced no bans as such and once again it couldn't really offend anyone. But this time around distribution was interrupted by litigation involving the sleeve.

Jamie Reid had come across a Belgian Travel Brochure, the cover of which was a cartoon of a family enjoying themselves in Ostend with accompanying speech bubbles. Jamie hit on the idea of reprinting the cartoon and inserting the words of the song in the bubbles. Legally, it is not possible to do this without permission which Jamie had not sought. Even the Belgian tourist office were sufficiently on the ball to issue an injunction against Virgin when the record was released. The record was in the shops on October 15 but an injunction was granted for infringement of copyright on October 20.

Virgin was obliged to withdraw 60 thousand sleeves immediately and the record was reissued in plain white sleeves. The Belgians also insisted that Jamie Reid destroy all the artwork associated with the Travel Company.

'Holidays In The Sun' was the first Pistols single to carry the writers' credit Rotten/Jones/Cook/ Vicious on the label.

The eagerly awaited first Sex Pistols album was originally planned for release in the summer of 1977 under the title 'God Save The Sex Pistols'.

Jamie Reid had again been commis-

sioned to do the artwork but for a variety of reasons, not least the band's penchant for changing record labels with some regularity and at the slightest provocation, which meant that this release date had to be postponed. So it was that on October 28 the album finally emerged with the eye catching title of 'Never Mind The Bollocks, Here's The Sex Pistols'.

The original album had been planned to run to 11 tracks with 'Submission' given free as a one-sided single and, as a bonus, a free poster was also included. Once again W.H. Smith and Woolworth gave a big thumbs down to the idea of stocking the record.

Such was the combined power of these two high street giants that Virgin Records toyed with the idea of re-pressing the album with the offending song, 'God Save The Queen', excluded. This, however, would have created all sorts of technical and financial difficulties and was dropped. The next problem was a legal one. Although the album had secured 125,000 advance orders which would guarantee it both a gold disc and a number one before its release – a first since The Beatles – there was some controversy as to whether the word 'bollocks' was obscene or not. Offensive to some it may well have been, but obscene?

Once again the long arm of the law intervened. Police all over the country carried out synchronised raids on record shops and confiscated the album under the existing pornography laws. In retrospect, it seems to have been a massive display of double-standards: the police saw nothing wrong in W.H. Smith and other leading high street retail outlets selling 'men's magazines' with naked women on the front but it was, apparently, a crime to display the word 'bollocks' on an LP sleeve.

A test case was brought against a gentleman called Chris Searle by W.P.C. Julie Dawn. The charge was that the shop had 'published' a piece of obscene shop window advertising and that the word 'bollocks' contravened the 1899 obscenity act. It was, quite rightly, thrown out of court and the word 'bollocks' can now be used with impunity.

The Sun carried probably one of their finest photo-headlines when they pictured Chris Searle holding aloft the album and saying the immortal words: "And the same to you."

As a result of this piece of 'legal history' the record was a smash and Virgin sent the group out on a tour of

radio stations and record shops to further promote the already top selling album.

During November 1977 the group signed a contract with Warner Brothers Records for the rights to issue their records in the largest market in the world, the USA. At the same time Virgin started to make plans for a US Sex Pistols tour to begin in March 1978.

That same month, after a sustained period of harassment by the police, Sid and Nancy were arrested on drugs charges. "It had got to a stage where they couldn't even go out of the flat without being got at," says Anne Beverley. "Every time they moved they'd be nicked. They'd seize this, that and the other but no charges were ever brought."

An opinion was being formed by those close to the group that Nancy was a bad influence on Sid and, by extension therefore, on The Pistols as a whole. Johnny Rotten had even discussed with Malcolm McLaren a plan to kidnap Nancy and smuggle her back to the USA. As it happened, on the day that the 'kidnap' was scheduled to take place Nancy spent all her time with Sid, never leaving his side, thus rendering the plan ineffective.

December was spent touring Holland and on their return, just before Christmas, they decided to perform a batch of UK gigs. They played a concert on Christmas Eve and on Christmas Day they performed at a party in Huddersfield for the children of local firemen. There were about 250 of them all aged under 14. Anne Beverley says that Sid had always had a soft spot for youngsters, especially when they got to the cheeky age, and the fact that the concert went well over time – with Sid singing 'Born To Lose' and 'Chinese Rocks' – seems to prove the point.

The planned concert for Boxing Day at the Lyceum in London never took place, so the gig at which Sid devoted much of his time to the kids was The Pistols' last ever live appearance in Great Britain.

By this time Warner Brothers were anxious for The Pistols to visit America. Feelings with The Pistols' entourage were mixed. "We were a bit unhappy about the tour," says John 'Boogie' Tiberi, who was now the band's tour manager. "It was an unknown quantity and we didn't want to rock the boat in England. Malcolm was dead set against the idea and I had my doubts.

56

Warner's original idea was just to pro-mote one huge live show but due to the press coverage and interest this was extended to 11. Then via the odd ban or two it was reduced to seven, still a lot of concerts. We obviously had to get visas for every-body so Malc and I hit on the idea of 'over-filling' in the application forms and including their criminal records."

Visa applications for the USA have sections for criminal records and Malcolm decided that if the US immigration department was informed of the wide variety of offences and misdemeanours committed by The Pistols over the past few years, then there would be little chance that they'd be allowed into the country. Herewith the criminal records that were filled in, with glee, by Boogie and Malcolm:

John Lydon: posses-sion of Ampheta-mines (fined £40); John Simon Beverley: assault on two policemen (discharge), criminal damage (discharge), taking of Ford Transit (fined £20), destroying policeman's handset (£10 with £4 com-pensation), possession of offen-sive weapon i.e. flick knife (for-feit weapon), assault on police-man (fined £50 with £25 com-pensation); Paul Cook: stealing property worth £900 (fined £60); Stephen Jones: breaking and entering (fined £1), theft of £143 (one year probation), (theft of eight ignition keys (fined £6), taking and driving away (fined £6), driving under age without licence or insur-ance (fined £8), charged under vagrancy act (fined £30), dam-age to plate glass window (fined £15 with £7.20 compen-sation).

Despite these somewhat unsavoury revelations the visa application forms were accepted and temporary permits were issued. McLaren's bold plan somehow failed.

All the formalities having been completed the group flew out to the States on Tuesday, January 3, 1978. The first engagement of the tour took place at the Great South East Music Hall in Atlanta, Georgia on January 5. The first words spoken on-stage in the United States were: "Hello, my name's John and this is The Sex Pistols." 57

This was to be the starting point of a most disastrous tour which culminated in The Pistols splitting up. Musically it was far from being one of The Pistols' best performances: Steve's guitar was out of tune and John's voice left a lot to be desired both in pitch and intonation.

One American, asked by the media outside the music hall about his overall impressions of the gig, expressed his disappointment that The Pistols hadn't urinated on anyone and remarked that it would have been an honour if they had. Taliesyn Ballroom in Memphis was the venue that provoked John's priceless remark: 'I'm not here for your amusement, you're here for mine," but was otherwise unnoteworthy.

Accompanying the group on the road was New York photographer Bob Gruen whose recollections include Sid deliberately slicing into his own arm with a flick knife in a roadside diner in order to live up to his name in front of some Texas cowboys. Randy's Rodeo, their first venture into Texas was highlighted by Sid wearing a huge plaster on his arm as a result.

The Kingfisher Club in Baton Rouge was nothing out of the ordinary but at the Longhorn Ballroom in Dallas a particularly persistent individual took to hassling Sid on-stage. The man later admitted that he'd been trying to provoke him and was, in effect, calling Sid's bluff.

Unfortunately Sid's bluff was easily called and after pretending to ignore the situation his patience gave out and he smashed the offending man over the head with his bass guitar.

The final concert took place at the Winterlands Ballroom, San Francisco on January 14, 1978. During the day prior to the evening's performance, John and Sid appeared live on a radio phone-in programme for K-San, San Francisco, a transcript of which subsequently appeared on the album 'Some Product'. At least John was live, Sid wasn't really in it.

The concert was a complete sell-out, 5,000 tickets sold in one day. It wasn't the best concert they'd ever performed: Johnny Rotten had flu and Sid was not even on the same planet. He fell over on-stage at least five times during the course of the evening and on one occasion the roadie had to hang his guitar back round his neck. At the end of the 14-song set John told the audience, "Ah-ha-ha ever got the feeling you've been cheated," and with that The Sex

Pistols were no more.

After the show, backstage, Paul and Steve had a blazing row with John. They wanted out, finally and irretrievably. John was shocked but agreed.

"What about useless?" he asked, indicating Sid. "He's your bloody mate, you sort him out," said Steve and Paul.

In this respect John Lydon signally failed in his duties.

* * *

Punk Rock Magazine in the USA summed up all four members of the band under the heading 'What They Are Really Like'.

Sid Vicious
Outgoing, loony, self-destructive, attention seeking, sexually conceited, basically a nice guy.

Johnny Rotten
Nasty, self-centred, socially immature with girls, likes to test people, stuck-up.

Steve Jones
Very quiet, a little reserved, street-wise, good sense of humour, illiterate.

Paul Cook
Shy, friendly, fun to be with, independent, stable and unaffected.

6

The Swindle, solo career and Nancy

Immediately after The Sex Pistols' final concert in San Francisco the band disintegrated and went their very separate ways. The split was irreconcilable.

Johnny Rotten, soon to drop the 'Rotten' and reassume 'Lydon', went straight into the arms of Virgin – the enemy as far as Malcolm McLaren was concerned – where he became a consultant A&R man with special responsibility for reggae bands until his new project, Public Image Limited, got off the ground. He'd always been a reggae fan and Richard Branson respected his knowledge.

Steve Jones and Paul Cook sided with Malcolm for the time being, travelling with him to Rio where they would hook up with former Great Train Robber Ronnie 'Syrup Of Figs' Biggs to try to make a record and film a sequence which would wind up as part of The Pistols' feature film, The Great Rock 'n' Roll Swindle.

Malcolm, aware that the tensions within the band had pulled The Sex Pistols apart forever, returned to London via Rio and issued the following statement: "The management, Glitterbest, is bored with managing a successful rock 'n' roll band. The group is bored with being a successful rock 'n' roll band. Burning venues and destroying record companies is more creative than making it."

Sid, virtually abandoned by his former friends, chose to go his own unsteady way.

After the gig in San Francisco he allowed himself to be abducted by a couple of girls who'd rushed the stage and whom he'd invited back into the dressing room. He was last seen heading off into the San Francisco night in their car. A day later he turned up in Los Angeles where he enjoyed his notoriety on Sunset Strip for a night before boarding a plane for New York in the company of John 'Boogie' Tiberi, The Pistols' roadie. Boogie had been charged with the impossible task of taking Sid to a safe haven in England, cleaning him out and delivering him eventually to Rio.

Sid's bad but predictable behaviour on the plane scuppered these plans. He collapsed in his seat after drinking too much and was taken off the flight in New York and put straight into detox.

On January 21, seven days after The Pistols' final gig, Sid's doctor, Bernard Gussoff, issued a press statement on the condition of the patient. "Mr John Ritchie, a self-admitted prior narcotics addict, has recently been on an aborted methadone programme. On Thursday January 19 in Los Angeles, Mr Ritchie took 80 mgs of methadone prior to boarding a plane and sustained an overdose while in flight to New York. He was brought to the Jamaica Hospital, admitted, and has responded well to immediate treatment.

"The patient has only minor complications of a flare-up of an antecedent asthmatic bronchitis. He insisted on being discharged today. At the time of his discharge he is asymptomatic, except for a cough, alert, fully orientated and afebrile. His blood pressure is 140/80, pulse 80. Mr Ritchie was given Valium to be dispensed by his road manager if necessary, and elixophylline. He has been strongly urged to have follow-up medical care and long range control of the narcotic problem."

Sid, of course, had other ideas. Immediately on discharge he was reunited with Nancy and the pair headed for Paris to recuperate and film a sequence for The Great Rock 'n' Roll Swindle. Nancy loved the idea of being with her rock star boyfriend in Paris, staying at a fancy hotel and the fact that the record company was footing the bill added icing to the cake. But the so-called recuperative trip to Paris soon turned into a nightmare.

Recuperating drug addicts are advised to stay within a familiar environment. Sid, of course, had never been to Paris before and the city soon

became a haven where his addiction and dependency grew worse. He took solace in smashing up hotel rooms and buying drugs, all courtesy of the record company. His relationship with Malcolm McLaren grew from bad to worse until they couldn't even stand to be in the same room together. Above all, Sid refused to work.

Julian Temple, directing the band's movie, had originally suggested that Sid sing a version of Edith Piaf's plaintive paean to lost love, 'No Regrets', but to McLaren's chagrin he refused. Days passed with expensive film crews standing by until a man from Barclay Records, The Pistols' European record outlet, suggested he record 'My Way' both for the film and to provide a new record. Sid's reaction to the suggestion was again typically negative; the song meant nothing to him. But eventually Nancy persuaded him to do it on the understanding that the lyrics were changed to reflect Sid's more robust image.

Steve Jones was also flown out to Paris in the forlorn hope that it might spur Sid into some sort of action. Julian Temple envisaged the song being recorded in a slow conventional orchestral style, lots of cascading strings, piano, French horns and a restrained rhythm section, but Sid wanted to do it his way. In the end a compromise was reached and the first verse was done the Julian Temple way and the second in the style of The Ramones. According to roadie Boogie, Sid was so far under the influence of drugs that the song was recorded piecemeal, a bit here and a bit there as and when Sid was capable of stringing together more than one line at a time.

Sid's visit to Paris was notable for one other incident. Although John Tiberi, also in Paris, denies it ever happened, towards the end of his stay Sid is alleged to have inflicted a serious beating on Malcolm McLaren which climaxed in a mêlée in an elevator of their elegant Paris hotel. The incident following a screaming match on the phone between Sid and Malcolm.

"Malcolm got very annoyed and rang down to Sid's room and started telling him, you know, that he was just a fucked up junkie and he had no future of any kind," says Julian Temple.

While he was talking, Sid gave the phone to Nancy and, dressed only in his motorbike boots and underpants with a swastika motif, entered McLaren's room and started kicking him. "He ran out of the room and 63 along a corridor with the laundry women going 'Oh Monsieur! Monsieur!' and trying to stop him. Malcolm got into the lift and then Sid got in and really started hitting him," adds Temple.

McLaren fled to London and there is no evidence to suggest that he and Sid ever spoke to one another again.

It seems likely that Sid's intense hatred of McLaren was due to Malcolm's unconventional way of handling The Pistols' career. Sid wanted to be a rock 'n' roll star; he wanted to play in a band. Temple: "He was totally infested with a kind of rock 'n' roll tradition by then, through Nancy and through The Heartbreakers, and his big gripe was that Malcolm would not let them play, and never let them be a rock 'n' roll group."

It was apparent to all involved with the film in Paris that Nancy was inseparable from her Sid. "I remember coming back one day," says Temple, "and she'd cut her wrists, there was blood all over the bed and she'd faked up a suicide attempt to really make Sid feel that he shouldn't leave her, even for a few hours, to do any filming."

For all his strange behaviour, drunkenness and over the top drug intake, Sid impressed Temple with his talents. "I believed that Sid as a performer had a unique possibility to present things that no-one else could present, I thought he was tremendous. His performance on 'My Way' was great."

Indeed, many still regard Sid's spirited rendition of Sinatra's classic torch ballad as the highlight of the Pistols film.

* * *

The Great Rock 'n' Roll Swindle came together in fits and starts and in many ways it was something of a miracle that it was ever made at all, especially considering the differing attitudes of all those involved towards the project and each other. Its storyline was based on 10 simple stages of how to 'con' one's way into the charts. McLaren himself became the star due to the decreasing enthusiasm of the band, Steve and Paul being the only members still slightly interested.

How much film was shot, how much wasted, and how much used to assemble and edit the final movie will never be known. Sting filmed a scene for the movie which he later withdrew because he had no desire to be linked to such licentious material. The famous cartoon sequence, 'Something

Else', was animated and put together but never used for anything more than a record sleeve. Sue Catwoman shot several nude scenes, but as she was under 16 at the time McLaren's discretion rather than his valour won the day and these scenes were cut. Money used to film complete live concerts was largely wasted as only odd songs were used. McLaren had shot scenes of his own but no-one was interested in using them.

The whole idea for the film, its execution, planning and eventual completion was a total fiasco, another exercise in how to fool all of the people all of the time. The band had little or nothing to do with the movie, they merely played the bit parts. Malcolm McLaren was the star with a semi-reluctant Steve Jones in tow. Sid was strictly motorbikes and 'My Way'. Johnny Rotten only appeared in concerts and TV interviews and Paul Cook was conspicuous by his absence.

It was released in the summer of 1979, 12 months later than scheduled, after two years of judicious cutting, editing and padding. Produced by Julian Temple the final version was eventually re-released, in its full 104-minute edition, for home video in 1982.

According to the blurb that accompanied the film's release, Malcolm's creed for the successful management of a rock group involved the following manoeuvres:

1. Establish an unlikely and controversial name, e.g. Sex Pistols.

2. Sell, hype, bully and pressurise the concept.

3. Do not play concerts, let the punters wait, don't give the game away.

4. Attempt to become the World's greatest tourist attraction.

5. Cultivate hatred and contempt; these are your greatest assets.

It was actually a formula for outrage but it worked.

* * *

Sid and Nancy returned from Paris in the spring of 1979. In April he told Record Mirror: "I'll die before I'm very old. I don't know why. I just have this feeling. There have been plenty of times when we've (he and Nancy) nearly died."

Around about the same time Sid bumped into Glen Matlock, his predecessor in The Pistols, with whom he'd remained on friendly terms, despite manufactured press stories of the supposed rivalry between the two bass players. Over a drink in the Warring-

ton pub in Maida Vale, close to where they both lived, it was decided that the best way to scotch the mutual hatred rumours was to perform a gig together, a decision that led to the brief existence of the first punk super-group – actually a contradiction in terms since one of the first tenets of punk ideology was that 'supergroups', like 'superstars' were redundant in the new age.

Calling themselves The Vicious White Kids, Sid and Glen recruited Damned drummer Rat Scabies and guitarist Steve New and, after some discussion, Sid became the vocalist. During rehearsals he was reported to be very impressed by the fact that Matlock could play bass guitar through an entire song.

"We called ourselves The Vicious White Kids on account of the fact that it was a sort of amalgamation of all our names: Steve and I were in The Rich Kids, Scabies had a part time out-fit called The White Cats, and Sid was Sid," Glen Matlock recalled.

The ad-hoc band arranged re-hearsal space at a warehouse owned by Eezee Hire in Islington. The room contained some dusty old PA cabinets and Sid came upon a brand new Fender Mustang bass guitar which impressed him so much that he made a secret vow to steal it. Assuming that a blatant annexation was preferable to subtlety, he picked up the Fender, walked confidently through the ware-house yard, past the office windows, and delivered it proudly to Nancy.

The following morning, the day of their first concert date, the VWKs turned up at Eezee Hire where their own gear was stacked away in the warehouse to load up and drive to the venue. During the latter part of the preceding day, however, the dis-appearance of the Fender had been discovered. Eezee Hire's answer was simple: if the bass guitar could not be found there was no way that the band were taking their own gear out. Sid caused some consternation among the rest of the group by promptly denying all knowledge of the theft or the whereabouts of the offending instrument.

Glen Matlock: "He was so convinc-ing, I would have believed him myself but for the fact that I actually saw him nick it. He was absolutely and totally believable. Anyway I could see we weren't going to get any joy out of Eezee Hire so I took Sid to one side and told him it would be better to own up and get the bass back, because no bass equals no gear of our own, and no gear of our own

Opposite top: **Sid and Nancy Spungen.**

equals no gig, and no gig equals no money."

After this typically Matlockian piece of home-spun logic, Sid rang Nancy and arranged for the bass to be returned, telling the hire people that he'd just wanted to borrow it to get the feel of it, and that it would arrive shortly in a cab.

The Vicious White Kids were allowed to load their gear onto the van and made preparations to leave.

As their van pulled out of the yard, the cab pulled in complete with Fender Mustang in a bin liner. It emerged dripping with paint. Nancy, whose preoccupation with black extended beyond her underwear, had painted it matt black polyurethane.

The setting for the group's concert was the Electric Ballroom in Camden Town and their set went down very well. It seemed irrelevant that they performed the same numbers three times over.

Nancy had become so involved with Sid and the music business by this time that she fancied her chances as a backing vocalist. However, she had such a dreadful voice that Glen, ever the gentleman, arranged for her microphone to remain unplugged. Nancy never even noticed.

This was the one and only Vicious White Kids' appearance. Shortly after the show Sid returned, temporarily, to the now defunct Sex Pistols in order to film further sequences for The Great Rock 'n' Roll Swindle. Indeed, the film's opening title sequence was shot in London in June 1978, the idea being that it would show the group (Sid, Steve and Paul) auditioning for a new front man.

These auditions just couldn't be taken seriously as the first guy to turn up celebrated the occasion by wearing a 'Johnny Rotten' rubber face mask. He turned out to be Tenpole Tudor who would sing two numbers in Swindle and go on to enjoy a patchy career with Stiff Records during the early eighties, including a number six single called 'Swords Of A Thousand Men'.

Sid's next and final contribution to the movie was the recording of the Eddie Cochran hits 'Something Else' and 'C'mon Everybody'. "When Sid was going to record 'C'mon Everybody' I was invited down to the studio," recalls Anne Beverley. "They had just gone through the number. It was early evening and I could tell he wasn't very happy so we took a break and went across the road for a drink. This seemed to relax him a bit so

when we returned to the studio he

was more in the mood. I think my dancing to the music in the mixing room so that he could see me did the trick. He did a fabulous version, the one that's on the record, in one take."

The final movie shots involving Sid included the now famous motorcycle scene which was a backdrop for 'C'mon Everybody'. Blink and you will miss Nancy's brief appearance at the beginning of the clip. Years later the BBC would use the clip on Top Of The Pops when 'C'mon Everybody' entered the charts.

* * *

Nancy Spungen had, for some time, been toying with the idea of returning to the USA and taking Sid with her. They had endured considerable harassment at the hands of the British police and they both felt that they would be better off in America. An added attraction was Nancy's wealthy family who would be on tap in case of emergencies.

They decided that after Swindle had been completed they would leave England for good. By this time Malcolm McLaren and Sid no longer saw eye to eye on anything, and the likelihood of The Pistols re-forming was becoming more and more remote.

As the day approached for Sid and Nancy's departure for New York, Anne decided to take some time off work so that she could be there at the airport to say her farewells. Unfortunately there were problems regarding Anne's time off and, what with one delay after another, by the time she arrived at Heathrow they were already checked in and on board the New York flight. Various friends of Sid and Nancy, including Mick Jones, were also at the airport so she wasn't alone and did, in fact, manage to get a message to the aircraft saying goodbye to her son.

In New York the couple found accommodation at the Chelsea Hotel in Midtown, already notorious as the hang-out of poets, Bohemians and drug abusers for more than half a century. The Chelsea opened in 1884 as one of the city's earliest co-operative apartment blocks but it was converted into a hotel in 1905. Thereafter its occupants included James T. Farrell, Robert Flaherty, O'Henry, Dylan Thomas, Thomas Wolfe and, from the rock fraternity, Janis Joplin.

During the early part of their stay Sid and Nancy were interviewed for a video documentary entitled Dead On Arrival about The Pistols' final tour of the USA. The interview shows Sid in an advanced state of drug induced

the interviewer's ques-
tions with any degree of lucidity. For
the most part he is asleep while
Nancy, evidently on better form on
the day of filming, answers questions
on his behalf. Their addiction was getting out of hand and gathering
momentum.

By this time Nancy was acting as
Sid's manager and through her old
contacts was able to get him some
work on the downtown Max's Kansas
City and CBGB circuit. These bookings, initially at least, gave Sid a new
impetus and various friends who were
musicians rallied around and provided
support. Mick Jones, who had also
arrived in New York by this time,
played lead guitar on as many gigs as
he could. Sid also played gigs with
Johnny Thunders and Jerry Nolan
from the now defunct New York
Dolls.

At least one of Sid's New York gigs
was taped and Virgin eventually
released an album, courtesy of John
Tiberi, which included versions of
'Born To Lose', 'Stepping Stone',
'Belsen Was A Gas', 'Something Else',
Thunders' anti-drug song 'Chinese
Rocks' and 'I Killed The Cat' which
was a short version of 'My Way' retitled because Sid had forgotten the
lyrics to the original song.

The money that Sid earned from
these gigs was immediately funnelled
into their drug bank to finance his
and Nancy's chronic addiction. Night
after night during the sweltering late
summer they would stumble around
downtown New York, visiting punk
clubs to score heroin before heading
back to their squalid bedroom at the
Chelsea Hotel to fix up together.

Whatever happened in bedroom
100 at the Chelsea on the evening of
October 12 and early morning of
October 13, will always be open to
speculation since the two people who
acted out the drama are both dead,
and the one who briefly outlived the
other was too blocked to remember
what happened anyway.

There are three contradictory versions of the events that led to the
death of Nancy Spungen.

Glen Matlock heard the first from
Stiv Bators, former lead singer with
Cleveland's The Dead Boys who was
in New York at the time of Sid's
death. He also told Alex Cox, producer of the movie Sid And Nancy but not
until after the film had been completed. Stiv Bators died in Pa
a motorcy

Leon, Sid and Nancy had been out in the city, sightseeing and shopping," says Glen. "They'd all bought folding hunting knives.

"The main reason for this was that, because of the Chelsea Hotel's situation and its apparent policy of turning a blind eye to drug addicts, there were easy pickings for muggers, rapists and general scavengers. Sid and co felt a little safer knowing that they could protect themselves should it prove necessary.

"An Italian drug dealer had been pushing all day at the hotel and Sid and Nancy had bought the whole stash. The problem was when it came to night time the dealer found himself without enough stuff to enable him to take care of his own early morning fix. He went to see Stiv in the hope of obtaining Sid's and Nancy's room number.

"Meanwhile in room 100 Sid had overdosed, having practically taken the entire stock that they had previously bought. He was out cold and in common with most drug over indulgence his breathing was so shallow as to create the impression of deep coma or death. The dealer arrived at the door and hammered on it until Nancy eventually opened it. He told her that he wanted to buy back some stuff so that he could fix first thing in the morning. Nancy told him to fuck off and turned to go back into the room. The dealer saw the hunting knife on a table grabbed it and lunged at Nancy. His aim was perfect and the knife was plunged into Nancy's stomach.

"Sid's prints would have been all over the knife because he'd only bought it that day. The drug dealer sees that Nancy is dead or dying, assumes that Sid is already dead and leaves the knife where it can easily be found. He is wearing gloves. He picks up the drugs he needs and beats a hasty retreat, never to be seen again."

Glen's story is given added credence by the fact that a report did reach the NYPD of an unidentified male being seen around the area of room 100 at about four in the morning on October 13.

The second version of events, hypothetical but logical, takes into account Sid and Nancy's oft-stated desire to end it all together. On the evening of October 12, Sid and Nancy, after consuming large amounts of drugs, decided that this would be the night for their joint suicide attempt.

For a variety of reasons they finished up arguing. Sid was already holding the knife and in the heat of

74

Backstage at the Vicious White Kids concert at London's Electric Ballroom, August 1978.
LEFT TO RIGHT: Glen Matlock, Nancy, Sid, Steve New and Rat Scabies.

the moment Nancy lunged at him impaling herself on it. Sid thinks she's dead or dying and, knowing that her part of the bargain has been kept, tries to overdose sufficiently to kill himself but fails.

The third version, again hypothetical but logical, is that Nancy killed herself deliberately. Sid had taken so much tuinol that he appeared dead. Despite all Nancy's efforts to revive him, no sign of life could be detected. While it would appear that slashing your own stomach with a hunting knife would be both painful and messy, it must be realised that the knife was brand new and razor sharp. Perhaps Nancy's sense of the dramatic ruled the day.

Whichever version you choose to believe, and there may well be others, the truth remains elusive. They are both dead. It is unlikely, however, that Sid deliberately killed Nancy Spungen. He was too much in love with her for that. She meant everything to him.

7

Love kills

Ever on the lookout for a good story involving delinquent behaviour by rock stars past and present, the popular press had a field day on the morning of October 13.

It was the day the world awoke to the news that Nancy Spungen was no more. She had been stabbed to death in her New York hotel room in what appeared to be a gruesomely macabre murder perpetrated, one was left to assume, by Sid Vicious, late of the unlamented Sex Pistols, her lover and fellow degenerate. The story had it all and more: sex, drugs and rock 'n' roll with murder for an added piquancy.

That same morning the New York Police Department charged Sid Vicious under his real name of John Simon Ritchie with second degree murder. After his arrest he was transported to Riker's Island Penitentiary and immediately admitted to the prison hospital's detoxification programme at Bellevue. Throughout the ordeal he was totally under the influence of, and dependent on, heroin.

When the news broke in London the commercial potential of the affair did not escape Malcolm McLaren. With his customary eagle-eye on the cash register he immediately went into production, and his shop Sex soon had a new line in T-shirts showing Sid holding a knife beneath the slogan 'She's dead, I'm yours.'

This display of supreme bad taste might explain why a number of the people interviewed for this book were scathing in their attitudes towards Malcolm McLaren. His well known adage might have been 'Cash From Chaos' but this was taking things too

far. Sid, according to depositions

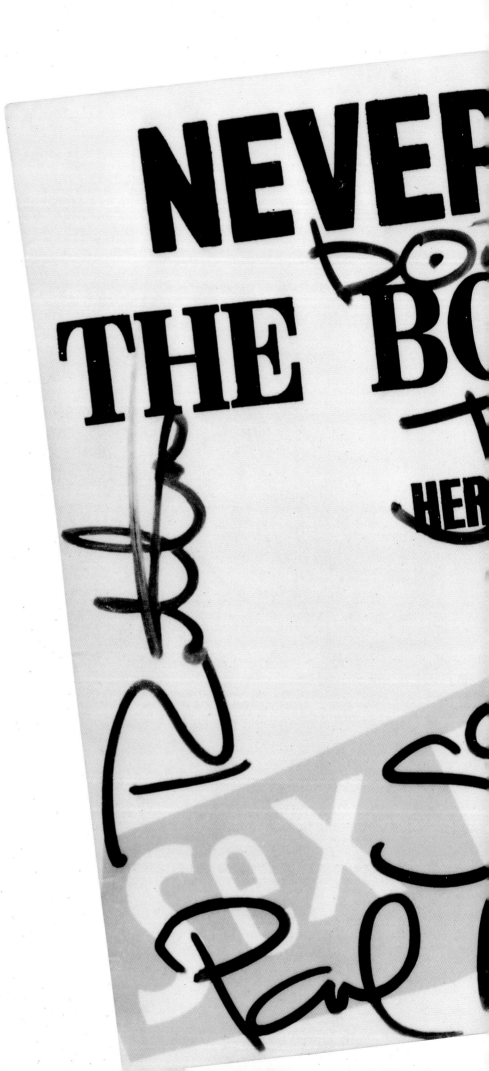

included with the lawsuit that John Lydon was subsequently to press on McLaren, wasn't even signed to Glitterbest, McLaren's company, because McLaren had neglected to sign up the 'new' Sex Pistols after Matlock was fired and replaced by Sid.

On hearing the news, Anne Beverley caught the first plane out to New York, as did McLaren. Anne lost no time in securing the services of an expensive law firm, Prior, Cashman, Sherman and Flynnput, who set in motion the wheels that would secure her son's release, at least temporarily.

To cover the cost of the high fees likely to be charged by a premier New York law firm, Malcolm came up with the idea of Sid recording an album with Steve Jones and Paul Cook, provided bail could be set. In the event this never happened and Virgin came up with $30,000 bail.

Sid, not unnaturally, was in a very bad state of shock, and would have been quite incapable of taking part in a recording session with his former Sex Pistols colleagues anyway. When he was arrested by the New York Police he apparently asked them to shoot him, to kill him because 'his baby was dead'.

Joe Stevens, a freelance rock photographer and one of the first on the scene at the Chelsea, had already told the press that Sid had admitted there had been a suicide pact and that Sid and Nancy had been planning to kill themselves for two or three weeks. Stevens later added: "There was blood everywhere when I arrived. Both his arms were badly cut."

During his stay at Riker's Island, where he was abused by fellow prisoners, Sid made the following statement:

"She's (Nancy) in my thoughts night and day. I wake up in the night reaching out for her, for her warm body which has always been cuddled up next to me for the last two years. I get into a hot sweat because I've been dreaming. I was making love to her again. The touch of her skin floats around in my brain driving me mad. Nancy in her sexy red and black underwear, the vision of her never leaves me. I could never have killed her. When you love someone as much as I loved Nancy you could never kill her. Life's almost impossible without her. I'm constantly thinking about the good times we've had together. Nancy was great because she and I were the same."

Whilst it is likely that some of these sentiments were straw clutching, induced by drugs or a convenient 79 mental rejection of the bad times, of which there were many, it is obvious that Sid and Nancy had a special bond that is only possible between people who've suffered their peculiar problems. Whether Sid and Nancy would have survived as a couple after rehabilitation and detox is open to conjecture.

Beyond the bare facts, the police report also stated that the NYPD were anxious to interview an unidentified young male who had been seen hanging around the couple's room around four a.m. the same morning.

According to Sid's version of events, he woke during the night and saw Nancy sitting up in bed fingering the hunting knife which they had bought earlier in the day. He fell asleep again almost immediately without speaking to her. His next recollection of events was waking up some hours later and seeing blood all over Nancy's half of the bed. "There was blood everywhere – on the sheets, on the pillow case, all over the mattress and on the floor leading to the bathroom. My first thought was that she had been killed!"

He then got up and went into the bathroom. He found Nancy slumped under the wash basin. After the initial shock he rushed into the corridor shouting for help. He then returned to their room and called the hotel reception desk.

"Get an ambulance up here quick, I'm not kidding!"

Within a matter of three or four minutes the police, not the ambulance service, arrived at room 100.

Sid sat on the bed completely dazed. It was later revealed that he had taken enough tuinol to kill a horse. He was immediately advised of his rights and accused of the murder of Nancy.

New York Police Dept: "Listen, kid, why'd you do that?"

Sid: "Why did I do what?"

NYPD: "Why'd you kill the girl?"

Sid: "I didn't kill her."

NYPD: "If you didn't kill her, why can't you look me straight in the face?"

Sid: "OK mate, I'm looking you straight in the face. I didn't kill her!"

The police clearly thought they were talking to Nancy's assailant and that Sid's denial was untrue. He was pushed face first against a wall, handcuffed and led away.

Nancy's body was tidied up and, after the post-mortem had confirmed the obvious fact that she'd been stabbed to death, she was flown back to Philadelphia to be buried there by her parents.

After Sid's initial appearance in court bail was granted and set at $30,000. This was posted by Virgin Records. If Sid was found guilty on the charge of second degree murder he could expect to receive a minimum sentence of seven years, including parole, whilst the maximum could be 25 years.

Although he wrote some songs in prison Sid was never to record again. McLaren's plans for an album went awry. Sid was released from Riker's Island in late November into the custody of his mother and a probation officer.

While Sid was on bail he found himself another girlfriend, Michelle Robison, and the couple provided each other with mutual support, though at the time Sid, on parole for allegedly murdering his last girlfriend, could hardly be described as an eligible bachelor. "He had this magic drawing power," the doughty Michelle is reported to have said.

Sid and Michelle were at Hurrah, a New York disco, on December 6 when a fight broke out which resulted in Todd Smith, brother of singer Patti Smith, being hospitalised after being cut in the face with broken glass. Sid, already on bail for a murder rap, was again arrested. Bail was again set

I go home once a week to have dinner with my mum." Sid Vicious,

Sounds magazine, October 1976.

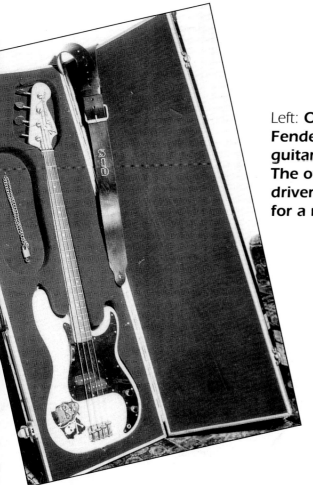

Left: **One of two white Fender Precision bass guitars that belonged to Sid. The other was given to a cab driver by Sid as payment for a ride.**

including the condition that he did not attend any night clubs or discos.

Anne Beverley and Michelle Robison were there to meet him on his second release in a matter of weeks. He was wearing a raincoat, a T-Shirt with 'I Love New York' on it and the inevitable jeans.

A party had been planned to celebrate his release but later that evening Sid retired early to bed and took a large dose of high quality heroin. He had been clean for the previous week and his body could not take it. Had he not been weaned off the drug, it is unlikely that it would have affected him as it did.

Sid died on the morning of February 2, 1979. The case of the murder of Nancy Spungen never came to trial.

Sid had told his mother: "Mum, Nancy is there on the other side waiting for me. If I'm quick I can catch the girl I love."

New York's Chief Medical Examiner, Dr Michael Baden, examined the body of Sid Vicious and said that he appeared to have died 'inadvertently'.

Sid's last wish was to be buried next to Nancy. This was not possible. The Spungens, to this day uncooperative, refused to reveal the location of their daughter's grave.

Anne Beverley had her son's body cremated and later, by chance, found out the burial place of Nancy. As a result of this she made a special trip to the Jewish cemetery in Philadelphia and scattered Sid's ashes over Nancy's grave, thus granting his last wish.

Sid's suicide note found in New York

From Gary to Sid: a legend is born

It was inevitable that the headline grabbing deaths of Sid Vicious and Nancy Spungen would be followed by hard nosed commercial exploitation on all fronts.

Virgin Records have always insisted that 'Something Else' was scheduled for release as a single before Sid's death. The record company have claimed that before the end of 1978 a release date of February 23, 1979, had been penned in. Either way, before the year was out Virgin issued 'Flogging A Dead Horse', a Pistols' greatest hits package, in October, and also 'Sid Sings', the album of tracks recorded live at Max's Kansas City in New York in 1978 by John Tiberi. The packaging of this album was an important element, and an illustrated inner sleeve and Sid poster were added as inducements to make this the ultimate Christmas gift for Sex Pistols fans. It was available from December 7 in the mid-price range.

Such was the interest in Sid that strong rumours circulated within the music press in the early eighties that a movie about his life was imminent. Hints were dropped everywhere and New Musical Express even ran a series of advertisements for Sid Vicious look-alikes to contact them with photos.

These rumours were substantiated when it became clear that a film initially titled Love Kills was to be the new project for producer Alex Cox. **84** Already famous for the cult movie

Sid and Nancy in Paris.

Gary Oldman and Chloe Webb as Sid and Nancy in the film of their life.

Repo Man, **Cox** and **Abbe Wool** submitted a story-line and script to movie companies for the planned film. The name was changed from *Love Kills* to *Sid And Nancy* because the former had already been used for a film and Alex Cox didn't want to cause any confusion.

Cox told NME in 1985: "We want to make the film, not just about Sid Vicious and punk, but as an anti-drugs statement, to show that the degradation caused to various people is not at all glamorous."

The selection process to find an actor to portray Sid was lengthy and arduous. Eventually, after much head scratching and soul-searching, a little known London actor called Gary Oldman was chosen for the part. With a film about the life of someone who has died recently it is essential that the actor who plays the title role has more than a passing likeness to the character he portrays. At first glance there were two disadvantages in using Gary Oldman: his age (he was already 27, a good six years older than Sid when he died) and his height (he was a few inches shorter than Sid).

In every other way he was perfect. Oldman's background was similar to Sid's, insofar as he was brought up in London and the guiding influence in formative years was his mother. His father, an alcoholic, was never there and so his mother had, more or less, experienced a similar situation to Anne Beverley.

But the most striking thing about Gary was his uncanny facial resemblance to Sid. After much experimentation with his hair to achieve Sid's spiked effect, he could have effectively passed as a passport double. His previously mentioned lack of height could easily be compensated for by clever camerawork when the film was actually shot. Tall actresses can always stand in 'holes' when appearing with short actors.

When Anne Beverley first heard about the movie she was antagonistic to the idea of running the whole story again so soon after the death of her son. "I just didn't want to relive it, and I moved heaven and earth to get hold of Alex Cox to try and persuade him to drop the project," she says.

When she eventually found out the name of the company who were to make and finance the film she initially came up against a brick wall. But Zenith, who had obtained the rights, eventually introduced her to Alex Cox, who was not only an excellent producer but sensitive to the feel-

ings of a recently bereaved mother.

The more that Anne spoke with Alex the more she grew to like the idea of the film. Her assistance in filling in background to the story would prove invaluable; indeed the padlock and chain worn by Gary Oldman in the film was provided by Anne and was the actual 'necklace' that had belonged to Sid.

Anne can recall the most heart-stopping part of the film: "When they shot the part when Sid came down the stairs in the 'My Way' sequence I was invited on to the set to watch the filming. As Gary came on I could hear myself saying, 'Sid is it really you?'"

It is evident that Sid underwent a character change after his involvement with both drugs and Nancy. This change, according to Anne Beverley, occurs in the film during the scene where Nancy destroys a telephone box, and she believes that Gary Oldman coped with this change admirably. It is fair to say that Gary took his portrayal of Sid Vicious very seriously, so much so that he starved himself down to Sid's weight. Actors and actresses are often so affected by the part they are playing, so totally immersed, that they actually become the character off the set as well as on. Thus it was with Gary and Sid. He wanted to be Sid.

He told Rolling Stone magazine: "I'd never really liked the script of Sid And Nancy. It put me off. It was inarticulate, monosyllabic, banal and probably extremely accurate bearing in mind the generation and type it was meant to represent.

"I was much more in favour of the idea that Alex Cox had developed to transform the script into the love story of two people... Sid Vicious and Nancy Spungen. This idea of Alex's was about all it had got going for it. In terms of actual dialogue it was quite terrible. I sincerely hope that Chloe (Webb) and I did as good a job as we could, lifting it off the pages and kicking it into some sort of shape on the screen."

Casting the part of Nancy Spungen was as exacting as that of Sid and after many screen tests a little known American actress, Chloe Webb, was selected. Chloe, later to achieve fame starring opposite Danny de Vito in the box office smash Twins, played the part of Nancy with a chilling likeness that was uncanny. She was very much Sid's equal in the film, not tagging along like some dumb groupie but an equal partner, especially in the last days when the film made it clear how difficult it was for

two addicts to clean their act up together. Instead of helping each other in this regard, they inevitably lead each other on to greater folly.

Anne Beverley: "They were a modern day Romeo and Juliet... if ever two people shouldn't have met it was Sime and Nancy."

Sid And Nancy was issued in 1986 to worldwide press acclaim: "Gary Oldman and Chloe Webb are almost too good for comfort... I felt trapped in the Hell of the characters they portray," said the Sunday Express; "Powerful and gruelling, a twilight world of needles, razors and vomit," said The Observer; and... "A savagely brilliant account of the last days of Sid Vicious," said The Mail On Sunday.

Sid And Nancy was blessed with a powerful story-line, and although the various ex-Sex Pistols seemed unhappy with the results, the only genuine faults were in tiny details that only keen fans would notice.

Glen Matlock was responsible for the faithful recreation of The Pistols' music in the film. Gary Oldman sang the part of Sid as well as playing the spoken character. Andrew Schofield ('Scully' from Channel Four's tale of the scouse rogue), who also sang his own numbers, was impeccable as Johnny Rotten.

Matlock, the only former Pistol with anything good to say about the film, feels that Rotten himself deserved a greater part. "I know that John got the right hump about the film but knowing him, as I did, it's probably because it's not about him," he says.

Alex Cox gave the film his best shot. He recruited Debbie Wilson, one-time member of the Bromley Contingent, to correlate the facts and handle the continuity and, wherever possible, he used Jamie Reid's artwork for background.

The Pogues, Pray For Rain, Glen Matlock, Steve Jones and Joe Strummer, who scored a Top 40 hit with his 'Love Kills' movie theme, all featured heavily in the soundtrack album and in 1986 Sid's favourite group, The Ramones, released their album 'Animal Boy' with the 'Love Kills' track especially recorded as a tribute to Sid.

* * *

Question: "Is there anything about the other English punk bands, the new wave, that you like apart from The Pistols?"

Sid: "I think The Clash are quite amusing sometimes. Joe Strummer makes me laugh. I watch him whimpering across the stage like a big pubic hair wafting about."

Question: "What about The Damned?"
   Sid: "The Damned aren't funny at all. They're quite sad. I want to cry when I see them."

Question: "Do you have any musical heroes? You can mention each other if you want."
   Sid: "Jefferson Airplane."
   Steve: "I thought I was your hero, Sidney."
   Sid: "Oh yeah, Fatty Jones."
   Steve: "There's shit in the dictionary!"
   John: "... and what's anybody doing about it, I mean..."
   Paul: "Never mind the testicles!"
   John: "Look at the state of the country, you can't do anything, you can't do a gig, you..."
   Sid: "Never mind your helmet!"

Sid: "Grown-ups just have no intelligence at all. As soon as somebody stops being a kid, they stop being aware. And it doesn't matter how old you are. You can be 99 and still be a kid."

"I've got absolutely no interest in pleasing the general public at all. I don't want to because I think that largely they're scum and they make me physically sick, the general public. They are scum.

"What I want to do is put something out that I like... and if nobody else in the whole fucking world likes it, I couldn't give two shits. If it doesn't sell one copy, who gives a fuck? The point is that it's what we want to do. We have fun making it, we have fun listening to it. I listen to our records a lot because I like them. I think they're good records. Otherwise I wouldn't have any part in them. I like our music to listen to as much as I like The Ramones.

"I think nothing has anything to offer, specially television and books.

"I don't like anything particularly."

"The Cash Pussies' first and only single '99 Per Cent Is Shit' was issued quite soon after the death of Sid Vicious. The cover picture featured a blood-spattered Sid, taken from one of the gigs on The Sex Pistols tour of the USA. The record's only saving grace was Sid's speaking voice both

before and after the song.

It goes to show that no matter how bad a record is, if it's packaged correctly it will sell. This record is now deleted and has become a rare collectors' item.

They say that everything The Sex Pistols touched turned to gold and because of continuing media interest, in the case of Sid Vicious, that remains true to this day. Sid's image is as young and striking now as it was in 1977 because it's the only image we've got. Leaving aside the drug-ridden pictures of him that resemble latter-day pictures of Elvis, the good outweighs the bad. His fellow Sex Pistols continue to change musically but they will age, gracefully or otherwise. Sid is still Sid the punk, as the owner of a tattoo studio in Blackpool remarked: "The 'Something Else' cartoon is the single most popular design. It's up there on my wall, good old Sid, he's kept the food on my table without even knowing it."

Exactly one year after his death a memorial march was held in London, with as many of the United Kingdom's punk rockers who could attend. Despite everything the truth of the matter is that Sid was well loved. As John Tiberi told us... actually no... as everyone we met told us... "You only had to be in the same room as the guy for a few minutes to realise he was a hell of a lot of fun."

Whatever opinions are held on Sid Vicious, he is here to stay. Long after The Pistols have been forgotten Sid will be up there with the best of them, Presley, Lennon, Bolan or whoever; they are now firmly in the same league.

According to Phillips Auctioneers in London a fully signed copy of 'Never Mind The Bollocks' is now worth twice the price of a fully signed copy of The Beatles' 'Please, Please Me' album. (It should be pointed out, though, that there are many more signed copies of The Beatles' LP in existence than The Pistols' record.)

'Then there was Sidney; what a natural terrorist, working in the pubs, making sure every gig the group played ended up in the most unpredictable bloody mess. He invented the pogo!" Malcolm McLaren (The Great Rock 'n' Roll Swindle – 1979).

Concert guide

The following is a complete concert guide to Sex Pistols shows performed with Sid Vicious as a member of the line-up.

1977

MARCH
5   **Notre Dame Hall, London**
21   **Notre Dame Hall, London**

APRIL
3   **Screen On The Green, London**

JUNE
7   **Queen Elizabeth River Boat, River Thames**

JULY
13   **Daddy's Dance Hall, Copenhagen, Denmark**
14   **Daddy's Dance Hall, Copenhagen, Denmark**
15   **Beach Disco, Halmstad, Sweden**
16   **Mogambo Disco, Helsingborg, Sweden**
17   **Disco 42, Jönköping, Sweden**
19   **Club Zebra, Kristinhamn, Sweden**
20   **Pingvinen Restaurant, Oslo, Norway**
21   **Ssamfundet Club, Trondheim, Norway**
23   **Barbarella's, Vaxjo, Sweden**
24   **Barbarella's, Vaxjo, Sweden**
27   **Happy House, Student Karen, Stockholm**
28   **Happy House, Student Karen, Stockholm**
29   **Venue Unknown, Linköping, Sweden**

AUGUST
19   **Lafayette Club, Wolverhampton**
23   **Roxy Club, London (did they or didn't they?)**
24   **Out Look Club, Doncaster**
25   **Venue unknown, Scarborough**
26   **Rock Garden, Middlesborough**
31   **Wood's Centre, Plymouth (as 'The Hamsters')**

SEPTEMBER
1   **Winter Gardens, Penzance**
17   **Virgin Records, Nottingham (album signing)**

During this period (March 1977 –
January 1978) several shows were
booked and then banned, cancelled
or simply not played. The gig
marked* was said to be The Pistols
best ever live show by none other
than Sid himself.

Before moving to America in the
summer of 1978 Sid played a one-off
gig at the Electric Ballroom in London
with The Vicious White Kids, a group
specially assembled for the night, on
August 15, 1978.

Between arriving in America and
Nancy's death in October 1978, Sid
also played a number of solo gigs at
CBGB's and Max's Kansas City.

To Sid

It seems like years, when told I cried
The night I heard Sid Vicious died
Born in nineteen fifty seven, fun and
young a punk in heaven.

The years that stopped at twenty one
were full and loud, a crazy song of
drugs and sex and frenzied shows with
laughter, tears, the highs and lows.

Spiked and black, wild forest hair, you
walked they stopped and turned to
stare.

Gentle giant the friend of we who
copy those we'll never be.

His face becomes a misty haze, con-
trolled; and deep like life, a maze.

Eyes of youth that stare you cold from
photos yellow, torn and old.

That look, that smile, he stole my life,
and married death a greedy wife

She robbed your soul denied our
dream

She haunts me now I wake and scream
Body drenched by cold sweat, I miss
the man I never met.